An Essay on the
Slavery & Commerce
of the Human Species,
Particularly the African

Translated from a Latin Dissertation,
Which Was Honoured with the First Prize
In the University of Cambridge,
For the Year 1785,
With Additions.

Neque premendo alium me extulisse velim.-LIVY.

by
Thomas Clarkson

TO THE RIGHT HONOURABLE WILLIAM CHARLES COLYEAR, EARL OF PORTMORE, VISCOUNT MILSINTOWN.

The dignity of the subject of this little Treatise, not any persuasion of its merits as a literary composition, encourages me to offer it to your Lordship's patronage. The cause of freedom has always been found sufficient, in every age and country, to attract the notice of the generous and humane; and it is therefore, in a more peculiar manner, worthy of the attention and favour of a personage, who holds a distinguished rank in that illustrious island, the very air of which has been determined, upon a late investigation of its laws, to be an antidote against slavery. I feel a satisfaction in the opportunity, which the publication of this treatise affords me, of acknowledging your Lordship's civilities, which can only be equalled by the respect, with which I am,

Your Lordship's,much obliged,and obedient servant,
THOMAS CLARKSON.

Contents

Preface

As the subject of the following work has fortunately become of late a topick of conversation, I cannot begin the preface in a manner more satisfactory to the feelings of the benevolent reader, than by giving an account of those humane and worthy persons, who have endeavoured to draw upon it that share of the publick attention which it has obtained.

Among the well disposed individuals, of different nations and ages, who have humanely exerted themselves to suppress the abject personal slavery, introduced in the original cultivation of the *European* colonies in the western world, *Bartholomew de las Casas*, the pious bishop of *Chiapa*, in the fifteenth century, seems to have been the first. This amiable man, during his residence in *Spanish America*, was so sensibly affected at the treatment which the miserable Indians underwent that he returned to *Spain*, to make a publick remonstrance before the celebrated emperor *Charles* the fifth, declaring, that heaven would one day call him to an account for those cruelties, which he then had it in his power to prevent. The speech which he made on the occasion, is now extant, and is a most perfect picture of benevolence and piety.

But his intreaties, by opposition of avarice, were rendered ineffectual: and I do not find by any books which I have read upon the subject, that any other person interfered till the last century, when *Morgan Godwyn*, a *British* clergyman, distinguished himself in the cause.

The present age has also produced some zealous and able opposers of the *colonial* slavery. For about the middle of the present century, *John Woolman* and *Anthony Benezet*, two respectable members of the religious society called Quakers, devoted much of their time to the subject. The former travelled through most parts of *North America* on foot, to hold conversations with the members of his own sect, on the impiety of retaining those in a state of involuntary servitude, who had never given them offence. The latter kept a free school at *Philadel-*

phia, for the education of black people. He took every opportunity of pleading in their behalf. He published several treatises against slavery,[1] and gave an hearty proof of his attachment to the cause, by leaving the whole of his fortune in support of that school, to which he had so generously devoted his time and attention when alive.

Till this time it does not appear, that any bodies of men, had collectively interested themselves in endeavouring to remedy the evil. But in the year 1754, the religious society, called Quakers, publickly testified their sentiments upon the subject,[2] declaring, that "to live in ease and plenty by the toil of those, whom fraud and violence had put into their power, was neither consistent with Christianity nor common justice."

Impressed with these sentiments, many of this society immediately liberated their slaves; and though such a measure appeared to be attended with considerable loss to the benevolent individuals, who unconditionally presented them with their freedom, yet they adopted it with pleasure: nobly considering, that to possess a little, in an honourable way, was better than to possess much, through the medium of injustice. Their example was gradually followed by the rest. A general emancipation of the slaves in the possession of Quakers, at length took place; and so effectually did they serve the cause which they had undertaken, that they denied the claim of membership in their religious community, to all such as should hereafter oppose the suggestions of justice in this particular, either by retaining slaves in their possession, or by being in any manner concerned in the slave trade: and it is a fact, that through the vast tract of North America, there is not at this day a single slave in the possession of an acknowledged Quaker.

But though this measure appeared, as has been observed before, to be attended with considerable loss to the benevolent individuals who adopted it, yet, as virtue seldom fails of obtaining its reward, it became ultimately beneficial. Most of the slaves, who were thus unconditionally freed, returned without any solicitation to their former masters, to serve them, at stated wages; as free men. The work, which they now did, was found to better done than before. It was found also, that, a greater quantity was done in the same time. Hence less than the former number of labourers was sufficient. From these, and a variety of circumstances, it appeared, that their plantations were considerably more profitable when worked by free men, than when worked, as before, by slaves; and that they derived therefore, contrary to their expectations, a considerable advantage from their benevolence.

2

Animated by the example of the Quakers, the members of other sects began to deliberate about adopting the same measure. Some of those of the church of England, of the Roman Catholicks, and of the Presbyterians and Independants, freed their slaves; and there happened but one instance, where the matter was debated, where it was not immediately put in force. This was in *Pennsylvania*. It was agitated in the synod of the Presbyterians there, to oblige their members to liberate their slaves. The question was negatived by a majority of but one person; and this opposition seemed to arise rather from a dislike to the attempt of forcing such a measure upon the members of that community, than from any other consideration. I have the pleasure of being credibly informed, that the manumission of slaves, or the employment of free men in the plantations, is now daily gaining ground in North America. Should slavery be abolished there, (and it is an event, which, from these circumstances, we may reasonably expect to be produced in time) let it be remembered, that the Quakers will have had the merit of its abolition.

Nor have their brethren here been less assiduous in the cause. As there are happily no slaves in this country, so they have not had the same opportunity of shewing their benevolence by a general emancipation. They have not however omitted to shew it as far as they have been able. At their religious meetings they have regularly inquired if any of their members are concerned in the iniquitous *African* trade. They have appointed a committee for obtaining every kind of information on the subject, with a view to its suppression, and, about three or four years ago, petitioned parliament on the occasion for their interference and support. I am sorry to add, that their benevolent application was ineffectual, and that the reformation of an evil, productive of consequences equally impolitick and immoral, and generally acknowledged to have long disgraced our national character, is yet left to the unsupported efforts of piety morality and justice, against interest violence and oppression; and these, I blush to acknowledge, too strongly countenanced by the legislative authority of a country, the basis of whose government is *liberty*.

Nothing can be more clearly shewn, than that an inexhaustible mine of wealth is neglected in *Africa*, for prosecution of this impious traffick; that, if proper measures were taken, the revenue of this country might be greatly improved, its naval strength increased, its colonies in a more flourishing situation, the planters richer, and a trade, which is now a scene of blood and desolation, converted into one, which might be prosecuted with *advantage* and *honour*.

3

Such have been the exertions of the Quakers in the cause of humanity and virtue. They are still prosecuting, as far as they are able, their benevolent design; and I should stop here and praise them for thus continuing their humane endeavours, but that I conceive it to be unnecessary. They are acting consistently with the principles of religion. They will find a reward in their own consciences; and they will receive more real pleasure from a single reflection on their conduct, than they can possibly experience from the praises of an host of writers.

In giving this short account of those humane and worthy persons, who have endeavoured to restore to their fellow creatures the rights of nature, of which they had been unjustly deprived, I would feel myself unjust, were I to omit two zealous opposers of the *colonial* tyranny, conspicuous at the present day.

The first is Mr. *Granville Sharp*. This Gentleman has particularly distinguished himself in the cause of freedom. It is a notorious fact, that, but a few years since, many of the unfortunate black people, who had been brought from the colonies into this country, were sold in the metropolis to merchants and others, when their masters had no farther occasion for their services; though it was always understood that every person was free, as soon as he landed on the British shore. In consequence of this notion, these unfortunate black people, refused to go to the new masters, to whom they were consigned. They were however seized, and forcibly conveyed, under cover of the night, to ships then lying in the *Thames*, to be retransported to the colonies, and to be delivered again to the planters as merchantable goods. The humane Mr. *Sharpe*, was the means of putting a stop to this iniquitous traffick. Whenever he gained information of people in such a situation, he caused them to be brought on shore. At a considerable expence he undertook their cause, and was instrumental in obtaining the famous decree in the case of *Somersett*, that as soon as any person whatever set his foot in this country, he came under the protection of the *British* laws, and was consequently free. Nor did he interfere less honourably in that cruel and disgraceful case, in the summer of the year 1781, when *an hundred and thirty two* negroes, in their passage to the colonies, were thrown into the sea alive, to defraud the underwriters; but his pious endeavours were by no means attended with the same success. To enumerate his many laudable endeavours in the extirpation of tyranny and oppression, would be to swell the preface into a volume: suffice it to say, that he has written several books on the subject, and one particularly, which he distinguishes by the title of "*A Limitation of Slavery.*"

The second is the *Rev. James Ramsay.* This gentleman resided for many years in the *West-Indies*, in the clerical office. He perused all the colonial codes of law, with a view to find if there were any favourable clauses, by which the grievances of slaves could be redressed; but he was severely disappointed in his pursuits. He published a treatise, since his return to England, called *An Essay on the Treatment and Conversion of African Slaves in the British Sugar Colonies*, which I recommend to the perusal of the humane reader. This work reflects great praise upon the author, since, in order to be of service to this singularly oppressed part of the human species, he compiled it at the expence of forfeiting that friendship, which he had contracted with many in those parts, during a series of years, and at the hazard, as I am credibly informed, of suffering much, in his private property, as well as of subjecting himself to the ill will and persecution of numerous individuals.

This Essay *on the Treatment and Conversion of African Slaves*, contains so many important truths on the colonial slavery, and has come so home to the planters, (being written by a person who has a thorough knowledge of the subject) as to have occasioned a considerable alarm. Within the last eight months, two publications have expressly appeared against it. One of them is intitled "*Cursory Remarks* on Mr. Ramsay's Essay;" the other an "*Apology for Negroe Slavery.*" On each of these I am bound, as writing on the subject, to make a few remarks.

The *cursory remarker* insinuates, that Mr. Ramsay's account of the treatment is greatly exaggerated, if not wholly false. To this I shall make the following reply. I have the honour of knowing several disinterested gentlemen, who have been acquainted with the West Indian islands for years. I call them disinterested, because they have neither had a concern in the *African* trade, nor in the *colonial* slavery: and I have heard these unanimously assert, that Mr. *Ramsay's* account is so far from being exaggerated, or taken from the most dreary pictures that he could find, that it is absolutely below the truth; that he must have omitted many instances of cruelty, which he had seen himself; and that they only wondered, how he could have written with so much moderation upon the subject. They allow the *Cursory Remarks* to be excellent as a composition, but declare that it is perfectly devoid of truth.

But the *cursory remarker* does not depend so much on the circumstances which he has advanced, (nor can he, since they have no other existence than in his own, brain) as on the instrument *detraction*. This he has used with the utmost virulence through the whole of his publication, artfully supposing, that if he could bring Mr. *Ramsay's* reputation into dispute, his work would fall of course, as of no authenticity. I submit this simple question to the reader. When a writer, in attempting to silence a publication, attacks the character of its author, rather than the principles of the work itself, is it not a proof that the work itself is unquestionable, and that this writer is at a loss to find an argument against it?

But there is something so very ungenerous in this mode of replication, as to require farther notice. For if this is the mode to be adopted in literary disputes, what writer can be safe? Or who is there, that will not be deterred from taking up his pen in the cause of virtue? There are circumstances in every person's life, which, if given to the publick in a malevolent manner, and without explanation, might essentially injure him in the eyes of the world; though, were they explained, they would be even reputable. The *cursory remarker* has adopted this method of dispute; but Mr. *Ramsay* has explained himself to the satisfaction of all parties, and has refuted him in every point. The name of this *cursory remarker* is *Tobin*: a name, which I feel myself obliged to hand down with detestation, as far as I am able; and with an hint to future writers, that they will do themselves more credit, and serve more effectually the cause which they undertake, if on such occasions they attack the work, rather than the character of the writer, who affords them a subject for their lucubrations.

Nor is this the only circumstance, which induces me to take such particular notice of the *Cursory Remarks*. I feel it incumbent upon me to rescue an injured person from the cruel aspersions that have been thrown upon him, as I have been repeatedly informed by those, who have the pleasure of his acquaintance, that his character is irreproachable. I am also interested myself. For if such detraction is passed over in silence, my own reputation, and not my work, may be attacked by an anonymous hireling in the cause of slavery.

The *Apology for Negroe Slavery* is almost too despicable a composition to merit a reply. I have only therefore to observe, (as is frequently the case in a bad cause, or where writers do not confine themselves to truth) that the work refutes itself. This writer, speaking of the slave-trade, asserts, that people are never kidnapped on the coast of *Africa*. In speaking of the treatment of slaves, he asserts again, that it is of the very mildest nature, and that they live in the most comfortable and happy manner imaginable. To prove each of his assertions, he

6

proposes the following regulations. That the *stealing* of slaves from *Africa* should be felony. That the *premeditated murder* of a slave by any person on board, should come under the same denomination. That when slaves arrive in the colonies, lands should be allotted for their provisions, *in proportion to their number*, or commissioners should see that a *sufficient* quantity of *sound wholesome* provisions is purchased. That they should not work on *Sundays* and *other* holy-days. That extra labour, or *night-work, out of crop*, should be prohibited. That a *limited number* of stripes should be inflicted upon them. That they should have *annually* a suit of clothes. That old infirm slaves should be *properly cared for*, &c.-Now it can hardly be conceived, that if this author had tried to injure his cause, or contradict himself, he could not have done it in a more effectual manner, than by this proposal of these salutary regulations. For to say that slaves are honourably obtained on the coast; to say that their treatment is of the mildest nature, and yet to propose the above-mentioned regulations as necessary, is to refute himself more clearly, than I confess myself to be able to do it: and I have only to request, that the regulations proposed by this writer, in the defence of slavery, may be considered as so many proofs of the assertions contained in my own work.

I shall close my account with an observation, which is of great importance in the present case. Of all the publications in favour of the slave-trade, or the subsequent slavery in the colonies, there is not one, which has not been written, either by a chaplain to the African factories, or by a merchant, or by a planter, or by a person whose interest has been connected in the cause which he has taken upon him to defend. Of this description are Mr. *Tobin*, and the *Apologist for Negroe Slavery*. While on the other hand those, who have had as competent a knowledge of the subject, but not the *same interest* as themselves, have unanimously condemned it; and many of them have written their sentiments upon it, at the hazard of creating an innumerable host of enemies, and of being subjected to the most malignant opposition. Now, which of these are we to believe on the occasion? Are we to believe those, who are parties concerned, who are interested in the practice?-But the question does not admit of a dispute.

Concerning my own work, it seems proper to observe, that when, the original Latin Dissertation, as the title page expresses, was honoured by the University of Cambridge with the first of their annual prizes for the year 1785, I was waited upon by some gentlemen of respectability and consequence, who requested me to publish it in English. The only objection which occurred to me was this; that having been prevented, by an attention to other studies, from obtaining that critical knowledge of my own language, which was necessary for an English composition, I was fearful of appearing before the publick eye: but that, as they flattered me with the hope, that the publication of it might be of use, I would certainly engage to publish it, if they would allow me to postpone it for a little time, till I was more in the habit of writing. They replied, that as the publick attention was now excited to the case of the unfortunate *Africans*, it would be serving the cause with double the effect, if it were to be published within a few months. This argument prevailed. Nothing but this circumstance could have induced me to offer an English composition to the inspection of an host of criticks: and I trust therefore that this circumstance will plead much with the benevolent reader, in favour of those faults, which he may find in the present work.

Having thus promised to publish it, I was for some time doubtful from which of the copies to translate. There were two, the original, and an abridgement. The latter (as these academical compositions are generally of a certain length) was that which was sent down to Cambridge, and honoured with the prize. I was determined however, upon consulting with my friends, to translate from the former. This has been faithfully done with but few[3] additions. The reader will probably perceive the Latin idiom in several passages of the work, though I have endeavoured, as far as I have been able, to avoid it. And I am so sensible of the disadvantages under which it must yet lie, as a translation, that I wish I had written upon the subject, without any reference at all to the original copy.

It will perhaps be asked, from what authority I have collected those facts, which relate to the colonial slavery. I reply, that I have had the means of the very best of information on the subject; having the pleasure of being acquainted with many, both in the naval and military departments, as well as with several others, who have been long acquainted with *America* and the *West-Indian* islands. The facts therefore which I have related, are compiled from the disinterested accounts of these gentlemen, all of whom, I have the happiness to say, have coincided, in the minutest manner, in their descriptions. It mud be remarked too, that they were compiled, not from what these gentlemen heard, while they were resident in those parts, but from what they actually *saw*. Nor has a single instance been taken from any book whatever upon the subject, except that which is mentioned in the 235th page; and this book was published in *France*, in the year 1777, by *authority*.

8

I have now the pleasure to say, that the accounts of these disinterested gentlemen, whom I consulted on the occasion, are confirmed by all the books which I have ever perused upon slavery, except those which have been written by *merchants, planters, &c.* They are confirmed by Sir *Hans Sloane's* Voyage to Barbadoes; *Griffith Hughes's* History of the same island, printed 1750; an Account of North America, by *Thomas Jeffries,* 1761; all *Benezet's* works, &c. &c. and particularly by Mr. *Ramsay's* Essay on the Treatment and Conversion of the African Slaves in the British Sugar Colonies; a work which is now firmly established; and, I may add in a very extraordinary manner, in consequence of the controversy which this gentleman has sustained with the *Cursory Remarker,* by which several facts which were mentioned in the original copy of my own work, before the controversy began, and which had never appeared in any work upon the subject, have been brought to light. Nor has it received less support from a letter, published only last week, from Capt. J.S. Smith, of the Royal Navy, to the Rev. Mr. Hill; on the former of whom too high encomiums cannot be bestowed, for standing forth in that noble and disinterested manner, in behalf of an injured character.

I have now only to solicit the reader again, that he will make a favourable allowance for the present work, not only from those circumstances which I have mentioned, but from the consideration, that only two months are allowed by the University for these their annual compositions. Should he however be unpropitious to my request, I must console myself with the reflection, (a reflection that will always afford me pleasure, even amidst the censures of the great,) that by undertaking the cause of the unfortunate *Africans*, I have undertaken, as far as my abilities would permit, the cause of injured innocence.

London, June 1st 1786.

Part 1:
The History of Slavery

Chapter 1

When civilized, as well as barbarous nations, have been found, through a long succession of ages, uniformly to concur in the same customs, there seems to arise a presumption, that such customs are not only eminently useful, but are founded also on the principles of justice. Such is the case with respect to *Slavery*: it has had the concurrence of all the nations, which history has recorded, and the repeated practice of ages from the remotest antiquity, in its favour. Here then is an argument, deduced from the general consent and agreement of mankind, in favour of the proposed subject: but alas! when we reflect that the people, thus reduced to a state of servitude, have had the same feelings with ourselves; when we reflect that they have had the same propensities to pleasure, and the same aversions from pain; another argument seems immediately to arise in opposition to the former, deduced from our own feelings and that divine sympathy, which nature has implanted in our breasts, for the most useful and generous of purposes. To ascertain the truth therefore, where two such opposite sources of argument occur; where the force of custom pleads strongly on the one hand, and the feelings of humanity on the other; is a matter of much importance, as the dignity of human nature is concerned, and the rights and liberties of mankind will be involved in its discussion.

It will be necessary, before this point can be determined, to consult the History of Slavery, and to lay before the reader, in as concise a manner as possible, a general view of it from its earliest appearance to the present day.

The first, whom we shall mention here to have been reduced to a state of servitude, may be comprehended in that class, which is usually denominated the *Mercenary*. It consisted of free-born citizens, who, from the various contingencies of fortune, had become so poor, as to have recourse for their support to the service of the rich. Of this kind were those, both among the Egyptians and the Jews, who are recorded in the sacred writings.[4] The Grecian *Thetes*[5] also were of this description, as well as those among the Romans, from whom the class receives its appellation, the *Mercenarii*.[6]

We may observe of the above-mentioned, that their situation was in many instances similar to that of our own servants. There was an express contract between the parties; they could, most of them, demand their discharge, if they were ill used by their respective masters; and they were treated therefore with more humanity than those, whom we usually distinguish in our language by the appellation of *Slaves*.

As this class of servants was composed of men, who had been reduced to such a situation by the contingencies of fortune, and not by their own misconduct; so there was another among the ancients, composed entirely of those, who had suffered the loss of liberty from their own imprudence. To this class may be reduced the Grecian *Prodigals*, who were detained in the service of their creditors, till the fruits of their labour were equivalent to their debts; the *delinquents*, who were sentenced to the oar; and the German *enthusiasts*, as mentioned by Tacitus, who were so immoderately charmed with gaming, as, when every thing else was gone, to have staked their liberty and their very selves. "The loser," says he, "goes into a voluntary servitude, and though younger and stronger than the person with whom he played, patiently suffers himself to be bound and sold. Their perseverance in so bad a custom is stiled honour. The slaves, thus obtained, are immediately exchanged away in commerce, that the winner may get rid of the scandal of his victory."

To enumerate other instances, would be unnecessary; it will be sufficient to observe, that the servants of this class were in a far more wretched situation, than those of the former; their drudgery was more intense; their treatment more severe; and there was no retreat at pleasure, from the frowns and lashes of their despotick masters.

Having premised this, we may now proceed to a general division of slavery, into *voluntary* and *involuntary*. The *voluntary* will comprehend the two classes, which we have already mentioned; for, in the first instance, there was a *contract*, founded on *consent*; and, in the second, there was a *choice* of engaging or not in those practices, the known consequences of which were servitude. The *involuntary*; on the other hand, will comprehend those, who were forced, without any such *condition* or *choice*, into a situation, which as it tended to degrade a part of the human species, and to class it with the brutal, must have been, of all human situations, the most wretched and insupportable. These are they, whom we shall consider solely in the present work. We shall therefore take our leave of the former, as they were mentioned only, that we might state the question with greater accuracy, and, be the better enabled to reduce it to its proper limits.

Chapter 2

The first that will be mentioned, of the *involuntary*, were *prisoners of war*.[7] "It was a law, established from time immemorial among the nations of antiquity, to oblige those to undergo the severities of servitude, whom victory had thrown into their hands." Conformably with this, we find all the Eastern nations unanimous in the practice. The same custom prevailed among the people of the West; for as the Helots became the slaves of the Spartans, from the right of conquest only, so prisoners of war were reduced to the same situation by the rest of the inhabitants of Greece. By the same principles that actuated these, were the Romans also influenced. Their History will confirm the fact: for how many cities are recorded to have been taken; how many armies to have been vanquished in the field, and the wretched survivors, in both instances, to have been doomed to servitude? It remains only now to observe, in shewing this custom to have been universal, that all those nations which assisted in overturning the Roman Empire, though many and various, adopted the same measures; for we find it a general maxim in their polity, that whoever should fall into their hands as a prisoner of war, should immediately be reduced to the condition of a slave.

It may here, perhaps, be not unworthy of remark, that the *involuntary* were of greater antiquity than the *voluntary* slaves. The latter are first mentioned in the time of Pharaoh: they could have arisen only in a state of society; when property, after its division, had become so unequal, as to multiply the wants of individuals; and when government, after its establishment, had given security to the possessor by the punishment of crimes. Whereas the former seem to be dated with more propriety from the days of Nimrod; who gave rise probably to that inseparable idea of *victory* and *servitude*, which we find among the nations of antiquity, and which has existed uniformly since, in one country or another, to the present day.[8]

Add to this, that they might have arisen even in a state of nature, and have been coequal with the quarrels of mankind.

Chapter 3

But it was not victory alone, or any presupposed right, founded in the damages of war, that afforded a pretence for invading the liberties of mankind: the honourable light, in which *piracy* was considered in the uncivilized ages of the world, contributed not a little to the *slavery* of the human species. Piracy had a very early beginning. "The Grecians,"[9] says Thucydides, "in their primitive state, as well as the contemporary barbarians, who inhabited the sea coasts and islands, gave themselves wholly to it; it was, in short, their only profession and support." The writings of Homer are sufficient of themselves to establish this account. They shew it to have been a common practice at so early a period as that of the Trojan war; and abound with many lively descriptions of it; which, had they been as groundless as they are beautiful, would have frequently spared the sigh of the reader of sensibility and reflection.

The piracies, which were thus practised in the early ages, may be considered as *publick* or *private*. In the former, whole crews embarked for the benefit[10] of their respective tribes. They made descents on the sea coasts, carried off cattle, surprized whole villages, put many of the inhabitants to the sword, and carried others into slavery.

In the latter, individuals only were concerned, and the emolument was their own. These landed from their ships, and, going up into the country, concealed themselves in the woods and thickets; where they waited every opportunity of catching the unfortunate shepherd or husbandman alone. In this situation they sallied out upon him, dragged him on board, conveyed him to a foreign market, and sold him for a slave.

To this kind of piracy Ulysses alludes, in opposition to the former, which he had been just before mentioning, in his question to Eumoeus.

"Did pirates wait, till all thy friends were gone,
To catch thee singly with thy flocks alone;

Say, did they force thee from thy fleecy care,
And from thy fields transport and sell thee here?"[11]

But no picture, perhaps, of this mode of depredation, is equal to that, with which Xenophon[12] presents us in the simple narrative of a dance. He informs us that the Grecian army had concluded a peace with the Paphlagonians, and that they entertained their embassadors in consequence with a banquet, and the exhibition of various feats of activity. "When the Thracians," says he, "had performed the parts allotted them in this entertainment, some Aenianian and Magnetian soldiers rose up, and, accoutred in their proper arms, exhibited that dance, which is called *Karpoea*. The figure of it is thus. One of them, in the character of an husbandman, is seen to till his land, and is observed, as he drives his plough, to look frequently behind him, as if apprehensive of danger. Another immediately appears in fight, in the character of a robber. The husbandman, having seen him previously advancing, snatches up his arms. A battle ensues before the plough. The whole of this performance is kept in perfect time with the musick of the flute. At length the robber, having got the better of the husbandman, binds him, and drives him off with his team. Sometimes it happens that the husbandman subdues the robber: in this case the scene is only reversed, as the latter is then bound and driven, off by the former."

It is scarcely necessary to observe, that this dance was a representation of the general manners of men, in the more uncivilized ages of the world; shewing that the husbandman and shepherd lived in continual alarm, and that there were people in those ages, who derived their pleasures and fortunes from *kidnapping* and *enslaving* their fellow creatures.

We may now take notice of a circumstance in this narration, which will lead us to a review of our first assertion on this point, "that the honourable light, in which *piracy* was considered in the times of barbarism, contributed not a little to the *slavery* of the human species." The robber is represented here as frequently defeated in his attempts, and as reduced to that deplorable situation, to which he was endeavouring to bring another. This shews the frequent difficulty and danger of his undertakings: people would not tamely resign their lives or liberties, without a struggle. They were sometimes prepared; were superior often, in many points of view, to these invaders of their liberty; there were an hundred accidental circumstances frequently in their favour. These adventures therefore required all the skill, strength, agility, valour, and every thing, in short, that may be supposed to constitute heroism, to conduct them with success. Upon this idea piratical expeditions first came into repute, and their frequency afterwards, together with the danger and fortitude, that were inseparably connected with them, brought them into such credit among the barbarous nations of antiquity, that of all human professions, piracy was the most honourable.[13]

The notions then, which were thus annexed to piratical expeditions, did not fail to produce those consequences, which we have mentioned before. They afforded an opportunity to the views of avarice and ambition, to conceal themselves under the mask of virtue. They excited a spirit of enterprize, of all others the most irresistible, as it subsisted on the strongest principles of action, emolument and honour. Thus could the vilest of passions be gratified with impunity. People were robbed, stolen, murdered, under the pretended idea that these were reputable adventures: every enormity in short was committed, and dressed up in the habiliments of honour.

But as the notions of men in the less barbarous ages, which followed, became more corrected and refined, the practice of piracy began gradually to disappear. It had hitherto been supported on the grand columns of *emolument* and *honour*. When the latter therefore was removed, it received a considerable shock; but, alas! it had still a pillar for its support! *avarice*, which exists in all states, and which is ready to turn every invention to its own ends, strained hard for its preservation. It had been produced in the ages of barbarism; it had been pointed out in those ages as lucrative, and under this notion it was continued. People were still stolen; many were intercepted (some, in their pursuits of pleasure, others, in the discharge of their several occupations) by their own countrymen; who previously laid in wait for them, and sold them afterwards for slaves; while others seized by merchants, who traded on the different coasts, were torn from their friends and connections, and carried into slavery. The merchants of Thessaly, if we can credit Aristophanes[14] who never spared the vices of the times, were particularly infamous for the latter kind of depredation; the Athenians were notorious for the former; for they had practised these robberies to such an alarming degree of danger to individuals, that it was found necessary to enact a law,[15] which punished kidnappers with death.-But this is sufficient for our present purpose; it will enable us to assert, that there were two classes of *involuntary* slaves among the ancients, "of those who were taken publicly in a state of war, and of those who were privately stolen in a state of innocence and peace." We

19

may now add, that the children and descendents of these composed a third.

Chapter 4

It will be proper to say something here concerning the situation of the unfortunate men, who were thus doomed to a life of servitude. To enumerate their various employments, and to describe the miseries which they endured in consequence, either from the severity, or the long and constant application of their labour, would exceed the bounds we have proposed to the present work. We shall confine ourselves to their *personal treatment*, as depending on the power of their masters, and the protection of the law. Their treatment, if considered in this light, will equally excite our pity and abhorrence. They were beaten, starved, tortured, murdered at discretion: they were dead in a civil sense; they had neither name nor tribe; were incapable of a judicial process; were in short without appeal. Poor unfortunate men! to be deprived of all possible protection! to suffer the bitterest of injuries without the possibility of redress! to be condemned unheard! to be murdered with impunity! to be considered as dead in that state, the very members of which they were supporting by their labours!

Yet such was their general situation: there were two places however, where their condition, if considered in this point of view, was more tolerable. The Ægyptian slave, though perhaps of all others the greatest drudge, yet if he had time to reach the temple[16] of Hercules, found a certain retreat from the persecution of his master; and he received additional comfort from the reflection, that his life, whether he could reach it or not, could not be taken with impunity. Wise and salutary law![17] how often must it have curbed the insolence of power, and stopped those passions in their progress, which had otherwise been destructive to the slave!

But though the persons of slaves were thus greatly secured in Ægypt, yet there was no place so favourable to them as Athens. They were allowed a greater liberty of speech;[18] they had their convivial meetings, their amours, their hours of relaxation, pleasantry, and mirth; they were treated, in short, with so much humanity in general,

as to occasion that observation of Demosthenes, in his second Philip-
pick, "that the condition of a slave, at Athens, was preferable to that of
a free citizen, in many other countries." But if any exception happened
(which was sometimes the case) from the general treatment described;
if persecution took the place of lenity, and made the fangs of servitude
more pointed than before,[19] they had then their temple, like the Ægyptian, for refuge; where the legislature was so attentive, as to examine
their complaints, and to order them, if they were founded in justice, to
be sold to another master. Nor was this all: they had a privilege infinitely greater than the whole of these. They were allowed an
opportunity of working for themselves, and if their diligence had procured them a sum equivalent with their ransom, they could
immediately, on paying it down,[20] demand their freedom for ever. This
law was, of all others, the most important; as the prospect of liberty,
which it afforded, must have been a continual source of the most
pleasing reflections, and have greatly sweetened the draught, even of
the most bitter slavery.

Thus then, to the eternal honour of Ægypt and Athens, they were
the only places that we can find, where slaves were considered with
any humanity at all. The rest of the world seemed to vie with each
other, in the debasement and oppression of these unfortunate people.
They used them with as much severity as they chose; they measured
their treatment only by their own passion and caprice; and, by leaving
them on every occasion, without the possibility of an appeal, they rendered their situation the most melancholy and intolerable, that can
possibly be conceived.

Chapter 5

As we have mentioned the barbarous and inhuman treatment that generally fell to the lot of slaves, it may not be amiss to inquire into the various circumstances by which it was produced.

The first circumstance, from whence it originated, was the *commerce*: for if men could be considered as *possessions*; if, like *cattle*, they could be *bought* and *sold*, it will not be difficult to suppose, that they could be held in the same consideration, or treated in the same manner. The commerce therefore, which was begun in the primitive ages of the world, by classing them with the brutal species, and by habituating the mind to consider the terms of *brute* and *slave* as *synonimous*, soon caused them to be viewed in a low and despicable light, and as greatly inferiour to the human species. Hence proceeded that treatment, which might not unreasonably be supposed to arise from so low an estimation. They were tamed, like beasts, by the stings of hunger and the lash, and their education was directed to the same end, to make them commodious instruments of labour for their possessors.

This *treatment*, which thus proceeded in the ages of barbarism, from the low estimation, in which slaves were unfortunately held from the circumstances of the commerce, did not fail of producing, in the same instant, its *own* effect. It depressed their minds; it numbed their faculties; and, by preventing those sparks of genius from blazing forth, which had otherwise been conspicuous; it gave them the appearance of being endued with inferiour capacities than the rest of mankind. This effect of the *treatment* had made so considerable a progress, as to have been a matter of observation in the days of Homer.

For half *his* senses Jove conveys away,
Whom once he dooms to see the *servile* day.[21]

Thus then did the *commerce*, by classing them originally with *brutes*, and the consequent *treatment*, by cramping their *abilities*, and hindering them from becoming *conspicuous*, give to these unfortunate people, at a very early period, the most unfavourable *appearance*. The rising generations, who received both the commerce and treatment from their ancestors, and who had always been accustomed to behold their *effects*, did not consider these *effects* as *incidental*: they judged only from what they saw; they believed the *appearances* to be *real*; and hence arose the combined principle, that slaves were an *inferiour* order of men, and perfectly void of *understanding*. Upon this *principle* it was, that the former treatment began to be fully confirmed and established; and as this *principle* was handed down and disseminated, so it became, in succeeding ages, an *excuse* for any severity, that despotism might suggest.

We may observe here, that as all nations had this excuse in common, as arising from the *circumstances* above-mentioned, so the Greeks first, and the Romans afterwards, had an *additional excuse*, as arising from their own *vanity*.

The former having conquered Troy, and having united themselves under one common name and interest, began, from that period, to distinguish the rest of the world by the title of *barbarians*; inferring by such an appellation, "that they were men who were only noble in their own country; that they had no right, from their *nature*, to authority or command; that, on the contrary, so low were their capacities, they were *destined* by nature *to obey*, and to live in a state of perpetual drudgery and subjugation."[22] Conformable with this opinion was the treatment, which was accordingly prescribed to a *barbarian*. The philosopher Aristotle himself, in the advice which he gave to his pupil Alexander, before he went upon his Asiatick expedition, intreated him to "use the Greeks, as it became a *general*, but the *barbarians*, as it became a *master*; consider, says he, the former as *friends* and *domesticks*; but the latter, as *brutes* and *plants*;"[23] inferring that the Greeks, from the superiority of their capacities, had a *natural* right to dominion, and that the rest of the world, from the inferiority of their own, were to be considered and treated as the *irrational* part of the creation.

Now, if we consider that this was the treatment, which they judged to be absolutely proper for people of this description, and that their slaves were uniformly those, whom they termed *barbarians*; being generally such, as were either kidnapped from *Barbary*, or purchased from the *barbarian* conquerors in their wars with one another; we shall immediately see, with what an additional excuse their own vanity had furnished them for the sallies of caprice and passion.

To refute these cruel sentiments of the ancients, and to shew that their slaves were by no means an inferiour order of beings than themselves, may perhaps be considered as an unnecessary task; particularly, as having shewn, that the causes of this inferiour appearance were *incidental*, arising, on the one hand, from the combined effects of the *treatment* and *commerce*, and, on the other, from *vanity* and *pride*, we seem to have refuted them already. But we trust that some few observations, in vindication of these unfortunate people, will neither be unacceptable nor improper.

How then shall we begin the refutation? Shall we say with Seneca, who saw many of the slaves in question, "What is a *knight*, or a *libertine*, or a *slave*? Are they not names, assumed either from *injury* or *ambition*?" Or, shall we say with him on another occasion, "Let us consider that he, whom we call our slave, is born in the same manner as ourselves; that he enjoys the same sky, with all its heavenly luminaries; that he breathes, that he lives, in the same manner as ourselves, and, in the same manner, that he expires." These considerations, we confess, would furnish us with a plentiful source of arguments in the case before us; but we decline their assistance. How then shall we begin? Shall we enumerate the many instances of fidelity, patience, or valour, that are recorded of the *servile* race? Shall we enumerate the many important services, that they rendered both to the individuals and the community, under whom they lived? Here would be a second source, from whence we could collect sufficient materials to shew, that there was no inferiority in their nature. But we decline to use them. We shall content ourselves with some few instances, that relate to the *genius* only: we shall mention the names of those of a *servile* condition, whose writings, having escaped the wreck of time, and having been handed down even to the present age, are now to be seen, as so many living monuments, that neither the Grecian, nor Roman genius, was superiour to their own.

The first, whom we shall mention here, is the famous Æsop. He was a Phrygian by birth, and lived in the time of Croesus, king of Lydia, to whom he dedicated his fables. The writings of this great man, in whatever light we consider them, will be equally entitled to our admiration. But we are well aware, that the very mention of him as a writer of fables, may depreciate him in the eyes of some. To such we shall propose a question, "Whether this species of writing has not been more beneficial to mankind; or whether it has not produced more important events, than any other?"

With respect to the first consideration, it is evident that these fables, as consisting of plain and simple transactions, are particularly easy to be understood; as conveyed in images, they please and seduce the mind; and, as containing a *moral*, easily deducible on the side of virtue; that they afford, at the same time, the most weighty precepts of philosophy. Here then are the two grand points of composition, "a manner of expression to be apprehended by the lowest capacities, and, (what is considered as a victory in the art) an happy conjunction of utility and pleasure."[24] Hence Quintilian recommends them, as singularly useful, and as admirably adapted, to the puerile age; as a just gradation between the language of the nurse and the preceptor, and as furnishing maxims of prudence and virtue, at a time when the speculative principles of philosophy are too difficult to be understood. Hence also having been introduced by most civilized nations into their system of education, they have produced that general benefit, to which we at first alluded. Nor have they been of less consequence in maturity; but particularly to those of inferiour capacities, or little erudition, whom they have frequently served as a guide to conduct them in life, and as a medium, through which an explanation might be made, on many and important occasions.

With respect to the latter consideration, which is easily deducible from hence, we shall only appeal to the wonderful effect, which the fable, pronounced by Demosthenes against Philip of Macedon, produced among his hearers; or to the fable, which was spoken by Menenius Agrippa to the Roman populace; by which an illiterate multitude were brought back to their duty as citizens, when no other species of oratory could prevail.

To these truly *ingenious*, and *philosophical* works of Æsop, we shall add those of his imitator Phoedrus, which in purity and elegance of style, are inferiour to none. We shall add also the Lyrick *Poetry* of Alcman, which is no *servile* composition; the sublime *Morals* of Epictetus, and the incomparable *comedies* of Terence.

Thus then does it appear, that the *excuse* which was uniformly started in defence of the *treatment* of slaves, had no foundation whatever either in truth or justice. The instances that we have mentioned above, are sufficient to shew, that there was no inferiority, either in their *nature*, or their understandings: and at the same time that they refute the principles of the ancients, they afford a valuable lesson to those, who have been accustomed to form too precipitate a judgment on the abilities of men: for, alas! how often has *secret anguish* depressed the spirits of those, whom they have frequently censured, from their gloomy and dejected appearance! and how often, on the other hand, has their judgment resulted from their own *vanity* and *pride*!

Chapter 6

We proceed now to the consideration of the *commerce*: in consequence of which, people, endued with the same feelings and faculties as ourselves, were made subject to the laws and limitations of *possession.*

This commerce of the human species was of a very early date. It was founded on the idea that men were *property*; and, as this idea was coeval with the first order of *involuntary* slaves, it must have arisen, (if the date, which we previously affixed to that order, be right) in the first practices of barter. The Story of Joseph, as recorded in the sacred writings, whom his brothers sold from an envious suspicion of his future greatness, is an ample testimony of the truth of this conjecture. It shews that there were men, even at that early period, who travelled up and down as merchants, collecting not only balm, myrrh, spicery, and other wares, but the human species also, for the purposes of traffick. The instant determination of the brothers, on the first sight of the merchants, *to sell him*, and the immediate acquiescence of these, who purchased him for a foreign market, prove that this commerce had been then established, not only in that part of the country, where this transaction happened, but in that also, whither the merchants were then travelling with their camels, namely, Ægypt: and they shew farther, that, as all customs require time for their establishment, so it must have existed in the ages, previous to that of Pharaoh; that is, in those ages, in which we fixed the first date of *involuntary* servitude. This commerce then, as appears by the present instance, existed in the earliest practices of barter, and had descended to the Ægyptians, through as long a period of time, as was sufficient to have made it, in the times alluded to, an established custom. Thus was Ægypt, in those days, the place of the greatest resort; the grand emporium of trade, to which people were driving their merchandize, as to a centre; and thus did it afford, among other opportunities of traffick, the *first market* that is recorded, for the sale of the human species.

This market, which was thus supplied by the constant concourse of merchants, who resorted to it from various parts, could not fail, by these means, to have been considerable. It received, afterwards, an additional supply from those piracies, which we mentioned to have existed in the uncivilized ages of the world, and which, in fact, it greatly promoted and encouraged; and it became, from these united circumstances, so famous, as to have been known, within a few centuries from the time of Pharaoh, both to the Grecian colonies in Asia, and the Grecian islands. Homer mentions Cyprus and Ægypt as the common markets for slaves, about the times of the Trojan war. Thus Antinous, offended with Ulysses, threatens to send him to one of these places, if he does not instantly depart from his table.[25] The same poet also, in his hymn to Bacchus,[26] mentions them again, but in a more unequivocal manner, as the common markets for slaves. He takes occasion, in that hymn, to describe the pirates method of scouring the coast, from the circumstance of their having kidnapped Bacchus, as a noble youth, for whom they expected an immense ransom. The captain of the vessel, having dragged him on board, is represented as addressing himself thus, to the steersman:

"Haul in the tackle, hoist aloft the sail,
Then take your helm, and watch the doubtful gale!
To mind the captive prey, be our's the care,
While you to *Ægypt* or to *Cyprus* steer;
There shall he go, unless his friends he'll tell,
Whose ransom-gifts will pay us full as well."

It may not perhaps be considered as a digression, to mention in few words, by itself, the wonderful concordance of the writings of Moses and Homer with the case before us: not that the former, from their divine authority, want additional support, but because it cannot be unpleasant to see them confirmed by a person, who, being one of the earliest writers, and living in a very remote age, was the first that could afford us any additional proof of the circumstances abovementioned. Ægypt is represented, in the first book of the sacred writings, as a market for slaves, and, in the [27]second, as famous for the severity of its servitude. [28]The same line, which we have already cited from Homer, conveys to us the same ideas. It points it out as a market for the human species, and by the epithet of "*bitter* Ægypt," ([29]which epithet is peculiarly annexed to it on this occasion) alludes in the strongest manner to that severity and rigour, of which the sacred historian transmitted us the first account.

But, to return. Though Ægypt was the first market recorded for this species of traffick; and though Ægypt, and Cyprus afterwards, were particularly distinguished for it, in the times of the Trojan war; yet they were not the only places, even at that period, where men were bought and sold. The Odyssey of Homer shews that it was then practised in many of the islands of the Ægean sea; and the Iliad, that it had taken place among those Grecians on the continent of Europe, who had embarked from thence on the Trojan expedition. This appears particularly at the end of the seventh book. A fleet is described there, as having just arrived from Lemnos, with a supply of wine for the Grecian camp. The merchants are described also, as immediately exposing it to sale, and as receiving in exchange, among other articles of barter, *"a number of slaves."*

It will now be sufficient to observe, that, as other states arose, and as circumstances contributed to make them known, this custom is discovered to have existed among them; that it travelled over all Asia; that it spread through the Grecian and Roman world; was in use among the barbarous nations, which overturned the Roman empire; and was practised therefore, at the same period, throughout all Europe.

Chapter 7

This *slavery* and *commerce*, which had continued for so long a time, and which was thus practised in Europe at so late a period as that, which succeeded the grand revolutions in the western world, began, as the northern nations were settled in their conquests, to decline, and, on their full establishment, were abolished. A difference of opinion has arisen respecting the cause of their abolition; some having asserted, that they were the necessary consequences of the *feudal system*; while others, superiour both in number and in argument, have maintained that they were the natural effects of *Christianity*. The mode of argument, which the former adopt on this occasion, is as follows. "The multitude of little states, which sprang up from one great one at this Æra, occasioned infinite bickerings and matter for contention. There was not a state or seignory, which did not want all the hands they could muster, either to defend their own right, or to dispute that of their neighbours. Thus every man was taken into the service: whom they armed they must trust: and there could be no trust but in free men. Thus the barrier between the two natures was thrown down, and *slavery* was no more heard of, in the *west*."

That this was not the *necessary* consequence of such a situation, is apparent. The political state of Greece, in its early history, was the same as that of Europe, when divided, by the feudal system, into an infinite number of small and independent kingdoms. There was the same matter therefore for contention, and the same call for all the hands that could be mustered: the Grecians, in short, in *heroick*, were in the same situation in these respects as the *feudal barons* in the *Gothick* times. Had this therefore been a *necessary* effect, there had been a cessation of servitude in Greece, in those ages, in which we have already shewn that it existed.

But with respect to *Christianity*, many and great are the arguments, that it occasioned so desirable an event. It taught, "that all men were originally equal; that the Deity was no respecter of persons, and that, as all men were to give an account of their actions hereafter, it was necessary that they should be free." These doctrines could not fail of having their proper influence on those, who first embraced *Christianity*, from a *conviction* of its truth; and on those of their descendents afterwards, who, by engaging in the *crusades*, and hazarding their lives and fortunes there, shewed, at least, an *attachment* to that religion. We find them accordingly actuated by these principles: we have a positive proof, that the *feudal system* had no share in the honour of suppressing slavery, but that *Christianity* was the only cause; for the greatest part of the *charters* which were granted for the freedom of slaves in those times (many of which are still extant) were granted, "*pro amore Dei, pro mercede animæ.*" They were founded, in short, on religious considerations, "that they might procure the favour of the Deity, which they conceived themselves to have forfeited, by the subjugation of those, whom they found to be the objects of the divine benevolence and attention equally with themselves."

These considerations, which had thus their first origin in *Christianity*, began to produce their effects, as the different nations were converted; and procured that general liberty at last, which, at the close of the twelfth century, was conspicuous in the west of Europe. What a glorious and important change! Those, who would have had otherwise no hopes, but that their miseries would be terminated by death, were then freed from their servile condition; those, who, by the laws of war, would have had otherwise an immediate prospect of servitude from the hands of their imperious conquerors, were then *exchanged*; a custom, which has happily descended to the present day. Thus, "a numerous class of men, who formerly had no political existence, and were employed merely as instruments of labour, became useful citizens, and contributed towards augmenting the force or riches of the society, which adopted them as members;" and thus did the greater part of the Europeans, by their conduct on this occasion, assert not only liberty for themselves, but for their fellow-creatures also.

Chapter 8

But if men therefore, at a time when under the influence of religion they exercised their serious thoughts, abolished slavery, how
impious must they appear, who revived it; and what arguments will
not present themselves against their conduct![30] The Portuguese, within
two centuries after its suppression in Europe, in imitation of those *piracies*, which we have shewn to have existed in the *uncivilized* ages of
the world, made their descents on Africa, and committing depredations
on the coast,[31] *first* carried the wretched inhabitants into slavery.

This practice, however trifling and partial it might appear at first,
soon became serious and general. A melancholy instance of the de-
pravity of human nature; as it shews, that neither the laws nor religion
of any country, however excellent the forms of each, are sufficient to
bind the consciences of some; but that there are always men, of every
age, country, and persuasion, who are ready to sacrifice their dearest
principles at the shrine of gain. Our own ancestors, together with the
Spaniards, French, and most of the maritime powers of Europe, soon
followed the *piratical* example; and thus did the Europeans, to their
eternal infamy, renew a custom, which their *own* ancestors had so
lately exploded, from a *conscientiousness* of its *impiety*.

The unfortunate Africans, terrified at these repeated depredations,
fled in confusion from the coast, and sought, in the interiour parts of
the country, a retreat from the persecution of their invaders. But, alas,
they were miserably disappointed! There are few retreats, that can escape the penetrating eye of avarice. The Europeans still pursued them;
they entered their rivers; sailed up into the heart of the country; surprized the unfortunate Africans again; and carried them into slavery.

But this conduct, though successful at first, defeated afterwards
its own ends. It created a more general alarm, and pointed out, at the
same instant, the best method of security from future depredations.
The banks of the rivers were accordingly deserted, as the coasts had

been before; and thus were the *Christian* invaders left without a prospect of their prey.

In this situation however, expedients were not wanting. They now formed to themselves the resolution of settling in the country; of securing themselves by fortified ports; of changing their system of force into that of pretended liberality; and of opening, by every species of bribery and corruption, a communication with the natives. These plans were put into immediate execution. The Europeans erected their forts;[32] landed their merchandize; and endeavoured, by a peaceable deportment, by presents, and by every appearance of munificence, to seduce the attachment and confidence of the Africans. These schemes had the desired effect. The gaudy trappings of European art, not only caught their attention, but excited their curiosity: they dazzled the eyes and bewitched the senses, not only of those, to whom they were given, but of those, to whom they were shewn. Thus followed a speedy intercourse with each other, and a confidence, highly favourable to the views of avarice or ambition.

It was now time for the Europeans to embrace the opportunity, which this intercourse had thus afforded them, of carrying their schemes into execution, and of fixing them on such a permanent foundation, as should secure them future success. They had already discovered, in the different interviews obtained, the chiefs of the African tribes. They paid their court therefore to these, and so compleatly intoxicated their senses with the luxuries, which they brought from home, as to be able to seduce them to their designs. A treaty of peace and commerce was immediately concluded: it was agreed, that the kings, on their part, should, from this period, sentence *prisoners of war* and *convicts* to *European servitude*; and that the Europeans should supply them, in return, with the luxuries of the north. This agreement immediately took place; and thus begun that *commerce*, which makes so considerable a figure at the present day.

But happy had the Africans been, if those only, who had been justly convicted of crimes, or taken in a just war, had been sentenced to the severities of servitude! How many of those miseries, which afterwards attended them, had been never known; and how would their history have saved those sighs and emotions of pity, which must now ever accompany its perusal. The Europeans, on the establishment of their western colonies, required a greater number of slaves than a strict adherence to the treaty could produce. The princes therefore had only the choice of relinquishing the commerce, or of consenting to become unjust. They had long experienced the emoluments of the trade; they had acquired a taste for the luxuries it afforded; and they now beheld an opportunity of gratifying it, but in a more extentive manner. *Avarice* therefore, which was too powerful for *justice* on this occasion, immediately turned the scale: not only those, who were fairly convicted of offences, were now sentenced to servitude, but even those who were *suspected*. New crimes were invented, that new punishments might succeed. Thus was every appearance soon construed into reality; every shadow into a substance; and often virtue into a crime.

Such also was the case with respect to prisoners of war. Not only those were now delivered into slavery, who were taken in a state of publick enmity and injustice, but those also, who, conscious of no injury whatever, were taken in the *arbitrary* skirmishes of these *venal* sovereigns. War was now made, not as formerly, from the motives of retaliation and defence, but for the sake of obtaining prisoners alone, and the advantages resulting from their sale. If a ship from Europe came but into sight, it was now considered as a sufficient motive for a war, and as a signal only for an instantaneous commencement of hostilities.

But if the African kings could be capable of such injustice, what vices are there, that their consciences would restrain, or what enormities, that we might not expect to be committed? When men once consent to be unjust, they lose, at the same instant with their virtue, a considerable portion of that sense of shame, which, till then, had been found a successful protector against the sallies of vice. From that awful period, almost every expectation is forlorn: the heart is left unguarded: its great protector is no more: the vices therefore, which so long encompassed it in vain, obtain an easy victory: in crouds they pour into the defenceless avenues, and take possession of the soul: there is nothing now too vile for them to meditate, too impious to perform. Such was the situation of the despotick sovereigns of Africa. They had once ventured to pass the bounds of virtue, and they soon proceeded to enormity. This was particularly conspicuous in that general conduct, which they uniformly observed, after any unsuccessful conflict. Influenced only by the venal motives of European traffick, they first made war upon the neighbouring tribes, contrary to every principle of justice; and if, by the flight of the enemy, or by other contingencies, they were disappointed of their prey, they made no hesitation of immediately turning their arms against their own subjects. The first villages they came to, were always marked on this occasion, as the first objects of their avarice. They were immediately surrounded, were afterwards set on fire, and the wretched inhabitants seized, as they were escaping from the flames. These, consisting of whole families, fathers, brothers, husbands, wives, and children, were instantly driven in chains to the merchants, and consigned to slavery.

To these calamities, which thus arose from the tyranny of the kings, we may now subjoin those, which arose from the avarice of private persons. Many were kidnapped by their own countrymen, who, encouraged by the merchants of Europe, previously lay in wait for them, and sold them afterwards for slaves; while the seamen of the different ships, by every possible artifice, enticed others on board, and transported them to the regions of servitude.

As these practices are in full force at the present day, it appears that there are four orders of *involuntary* slaves on the African continent; of [33]*convicts*; of *prisoners of war*; of those, who are publickly seized by virtue of the *authority* of their prince; and of those, who are privately *kidnapped* by individuals.

It remains only to observe on this head, that in the sale and purchase of these the African commerce or *Slave Trade* consists; that they are delivered to the merchants of Europe in exchange for their various commodities; that these transport them to their colonies in the west, where their *slavery* takes place; and that a fifth order arises there, composed of all such as are born to the native Africans, after their transportation and slavery have commenced.

Having thus explained as much of the history of modern servitude, as is sufficient for the prosecution of our design, we should have closed our account here, but that a work, just published, has furnished us with a singular anecdote of the colonists of a neighbouring nation, which we cannot but relate. The learned [34]author, having described the method which the Dutch colonists at the Cape make use of to take the Hottentots and enslave them, takes occasion, in many subsequent parts of the work, to mention the dreadful effects of the practice of slavery; which, as he justly remarks, "leads to all manner of misdemeanours and wickedness. Pregnant women," says he, "and children in their tenderest years, were not at this time, neither indeed are they ever, exempt from the effects of the hatred and spirit of vengeance constantly harboured by the colonists, with respect to the [35]Boshies-man nation; *excepting such indeed as are marked out to be carried away into bondage.*

"Does a colonist at any time get sight of a Boshies-man, he takes fire immediately, and spirits up his horse and dogs, in order to hunt him with more ardour and fury than he would a wolf, or any other wild beast? On an open plain, a few colonists on horseback are always sure to get the better of the greatest number of Boshies-men that can be brought together; as the former always keep at the distance of about an hundred, or an hundred and fifty paces (just as they find it convenient) and charging their heavy fire-arms with a very large kind of shot, jump off their horses, and rest their pieces in their usual manner on their ramrods, in order that they may shoot with the greater certainty; so that the balls discharged by them will sometimes, as I have been assured, go through the bodies of six, seven, or eight of the enemy at a time, especially as these latter know no better than to keep close together in a body."-

"And not only is the capture of the Hottentots considered by them merely as a party of pleasure, but in cold blood they destroy the bands which nature has knit between their husbands, and their wives and children, &c."

With what horrour do these passages seem to strike us! What indignation do they seem to raise in our breasts, when we reflect, that a part of the human species are considered as *game*, and that *parties of pleasure* are made for their *destruction*! The lion does not imbrue his claws in blood, unless called upon by hunger, or provoked by interruption; whereas the merciless Dutch, more savage than the brutes themselves, not only murder their fellow-creatures without any provocation or necessity, but even make a diversion of their sufferings, and enjoy their pain.

Part 2:
The African Commerce, or Slave Trade

Chapter 1

As we explained the History of Slavery in the first part of this Essay, as far as it was necessary for our purpose, we shall now take the question into consideration, which we proposed at first as the subject of our inquiry, viz. how far the commerce and slavery of the human species, as revived by some of the nations of Europe in the persons of the unfortunate Africans, and as revived, in a great measure, on the principles of antiquity, are consistent with the laws of nature, or the common notions of equity, as established among men.

This question resolves itself into two separate parts for discussion, into *the African commerce (as explained in the history of slavery)* and *the subsequent slavery in the colonies, as founded on the equity of the commerce*. The former, of course, will be first examined. For this purpose we shall inquire into the rise, nature, and design of government. Such an inquiry will be particularly useful in the present place; it will afford us that general knowledge of subordination and liberty, which is necessary in the case before us, and will be found, as it were, a source, to which we may frequently refer for many and valuable arguments.

It appears that mankind were originally free, and that they possessed an equal right to the soil and produce of the earth. For proof of this, we need only appeal to the *divine* writings; to the *golden age* of the poets, which, like other fables of the times, had its origin in truth; and to the institution of the *Saturnalia*, and of other similar festivals; all of which are so many monuments of this original equality of men. Hence then there was no rank, no distinction, no superiour. Every man wandered where he chose, changing his residence, as a spot attracted his fancy, or suited his convenience, uncontrouled by his neighbour, unconnected with any but his family. Hence also (as every thing was common) he collected what he chose without injury, and enjoyed without injury what he had collected. Such was the first situation of mankind;[36] a state of *dissociation* and *independence*.

In this dissociated state it is impossible that men could have long continued. The dangers to which they must have frequently been exposed, by the attacks of fierce and rapacious beasts, by the proedatory attempts of their own species, and by the disputes of contiguous and independent families; these, together with their inability to defend, themselves, on many such occasions, must have incited them to unite. Hence then was *society* formed on the grand principles of preservation and defence: and as these principles began to operate, in the different parts of the earth, where the different families had roamed, a great number of these *societies* began to be formed and established; which, taking to themselves particular names from particular occurrences, began to be perfectly distinct from one another.

As the individuals, of whom these societies were composed, had associated only for their defence, so they experienced, at first, no change in their condition. They were still independent and free; they were still without discipline or laws; they had every thing still in common; they pursued the same, manner of life; wandering only, in *herds*, as the earth gave them or refused them sustenance, and doing, as a *publick body*, what they had been accustomed to do as *individuals* before. This was the exact situation of the Getæ and Scythians,[37] of the Lybians and Goetulians[38] of the Italian Aborigines,[39] and of the Huns and Alans.[40] They had left their original state of *dissociation*, and had stepped into that, which has been just described. Thus was the second situation of men a state of *independent society*.

Having thus joined themselves together, and having formed themselves into several large and distinct bodies, they could not fail of submitting soon to a more considerable change. Their numbers must have rapidly increased, and their societies, in process of time, have become so populous, as frequently to have experienced the want of subsistence, and many of the commotions and tumults of intestine strife. For these inconveniences however there were remedies to be found. *Agriculture* would furnish them with that subsistence and support, which the earth, from the rapid increase of its inhabitants, had become unable spontaneously to produce. An *assignation* of *property* would not only enforce an application, but excite an emulation, to labour; and *government* would at once afford a security to the acquisitions of the industrious, and heal the intestine disorders of the community, by the introduction of laws.

Such then were the remedies, that were gradually applied. The *societies*, which had hitherto seen their members, undistinguished either by authority or rank, admitted now of magistratical pre-eminence.

They were divided into tribes; to every tribe was allotted a particular district for its support, and to every individual his particular spot. The Germans,[41] who consisted of many and various nations, were exactly in this situation. They had advanced a step beyond the Scythians, Goetulians, and those, whom we described before; and thus was the third situation of mankind a state of *subordinate society*.

Chapter 2

As we have thus traced the situation of man from unbounded liberty to subordination, it will be proper to carry our inquiries farther, and to consider, who first obtained the pre-eminence in these *primoeval societies*, and by what particular methods it was obtained.

There were only two ways, by which such an event could have been produced, by *compulsion* or *consent*. When mankind first saw the necessity of government, it is probable that many had conceived the desire of ruling. To be placed in a new situation, to be taken from the common herd, to be the first, distinguished among men, were thoughts, that must have had their charms. Let us suppose then, that these thoughts had worked so unusually on the passions of any particular individual, as to have driven him to the extravagant design of obtaining the preeminence by force. How could his design have been accomplished? How could he forcibly have usurped the jurisdiction at a time, when, all being equally free, there was not a single person, whose assistance he could command? Add to this, that, in a state of universal liberty, force had been repaid by force, and the attempt had been fatal to the usurper.

As *empire* then could never have been gained at first by *compulsion*, so it could only have been obtained by *consent*; and as men were then going to make an important sacrifice, for the sake of their *mutual* happiness, so he alone could have obtained it, (not whose *ambition* had greatly distinguished him from the rest) but in whose *wisdom, justice, prudence*, and *virtue*, the whole community could confide.

To confirm this reasoning, we shall appeal, as before, to facts; and shall consult therefore the history of those nations, which having just left their former state of *independent society*, were the very people that established *subordination* and *government*.

The commentaries of Cæsar afford us the following accounts of the ancient Gauls. When any of their kings, either by death, or deposition, made a vacancy in the regal office, the whole nation was immediately convened for the appointment of a successor. In these national conventions were the regal offices conferred. Every individual had a voice on the occasion, and every individual was free. The person upon whom the general approbation appeared to fall, was immediately advanced to pre-eminence in the state. He was uniformly one, whose actions had made him eminent; whose conduct had gained him previous applause; whose valour the very assembly, that elected him, had themselves witnessed in the field; whose prudence, wisdom and justice, having rendered him signally serviceable, had endeared him to his tribe. For this reason, their kingdoms were not hereditary; the son did not always inherit the virtues of the sire; and they were determined that he alone should possess authority, in whose virtues they could confide. Nor was this all. So sensible were they of the important sacrifice they had made; so extremely jealous even of the name of superiority and power, that they limited, by a variety of laws, the authority of the very person, whom they had just elected, from a confidence of his integrity; Ambiorix himself confessing, "that his people had as much power over him, as he could possibly have over his people."

The same custom, as appears from Tacitus, prevailed also among the Germans. They had their national councils, like the Gauls; in which the regal and ducal offices were confirmed according to the majority of voices. They elected also, on these occasions, those only, whom their virtue, by repeated trial, had unequivocally distinguished from the rest; and they limited their authority so far, as neither to leave them the power of inflicting imprisonment or stripes, nor of exercising any penal jurisdiction. But as punishment was necessary in a state of civil society, "it was permitted to the priests alone, that it might appear to have been inflicted, by the order of the gods, and not by any superiour authority in man."

The accounts which we have thus given of the ancient Germans and Gauls, will be found also to be equally true of those people, which had arrived at the same state of subordinate society. We might appeal, for a testimony of this, to the history of the Goths; to the history of the Franks and Saxons; to, the history, in short, of all those nations, from which the different governments, now conspicuous in Europe, have undeniably sprung. And we might appeal, as a farther proof, to the Americans, who are represented by many of the moderns, from their own ocular testimony, as observing the same customs at the present day.

CLARKSON

It remains only to observe, that as these customs prevailed among the different nations described, in their early state of subordinate society, and as they were moreover the customs of their respective ancestors, it appears that they must have been handed down, both by tradition and use, from the first introduction of *government*.

Chapter 3

We may now deduce those general maxims concerning *subordination*, and *liberty*, which we mentioned to have been essentially connected with the subject, and which some, from speculation only, and without any allusion to facts, have been bold enough to deny.

It appears first, that *liberty* is a *natural*, and *government* an *adventitious* right, because all men were originally free.

It appears secondly, that government is a *contract*[42] because, in these primeval subordinate societies, we have seen it voluntarily conferred on the one hand, and accepted on the other. We have seen it subject to various restrictions. We have seen its articles, which could then only be written by tradition and use, as perfect and binding as those, which are now committed to letters. We have seen it, in short, partaking of the *federal* nature, as much as it could in a state, which wanted the means of recording its transactions.

It appear thirdly, that the grand object of the *contrast*, is the *happiness* of the people; because they gave the supremacy to him alone, who had been conspicuous for the splendour of his abilities, or the integrity of his life: that the power of the multitude being directed by the *wisdom* and *justice* of the prince, they might experience the most effectual protection from injury, the highest advantages of society, the greatest possible *happiness*.

Chapter 4

Having now collected the materials that are necessary for the prosecution of our design, we shall immediately enter upon the discussion.

If any man had originally been endued with power, as with other faculties, so that the rest of mankind had discovered in themselves an *innate necessity* of obeying this particular person; it is evident that he and his descendants, from the superiority of their nature, would have had a claim upon men for obedience, and a natural right to command: but as the right to empire is *adventitious*; as all were originally free; as nature made every man's body and mind *his own*; it is evident that no just man can be consigned to *slavery*, without his own *consent*.

Neither can men, by the same principles, be considered as lands, goods, or houses, among *possessions*. It is necessary that all *property* should be inferiour to its *possessor*. But how does the *slave* differ from his *master*, but by *chance*? For though the mark, with which the latter is pleased to brand him, shews, at the first sight, the difference of their *fortune*; what mark can be found in his *nature*, that can warrant a distinction?

To this consideration we shall add the following, that if men can justly become the property of each other, their children, like the offspring of cattle, must inherit their *paternal* lot. Now, as the actions of the father and the child must be thus at the sole disposal of their common master, it is evident, that the *authority* of the one, as a *parent*, and the *duty* of the other, as a *child*, must be instantly annihilated; rights and obligations, which, as they are sounded in nature, are implanted in our feelings, and are established by the voice of God, must contain in their annihilation a solid argument to prove, that there cannot be any *property* whatever in the *human species*.

We may consider also, as a farther confirmation, that it is impossible, in the nature of things, that *liberty* can be *bought* or *sold*! It is neither *saleable*, nor *purchasable*. For if any one man can have an absolute property in the liberty of another, or, in other words, if he, who is called a *master*, can have a *just* right to command the actions of him, who is called a *slave*, it is evident that the latter cannot be accountable for those crimes, which the former may order him to commit. Now as every reasonable being is accountable for his actions, it is evident, that such a right cannot *justly* exist, and that human liberty, of course, is beyond the possibility either of *sale* or *purchase*. Add to this, that, whenever you sell the liberty of a man, you have the power only of alluding to the *body*: the *mind* cannot be confined or bound: it will be free, though its mansion be beset with chains. But if, in every sale of the *human species*, you are under the necessity of considering your slave in this abstracted light; of alluding only to the body, and of making no allusion to the mind; you are under the necessity also of treating him, in the same moment, as a *brute*, and of abusing therefore that nature, which cannot otherwise be considered, than in the double capacity of *soul* and *body*.

But some person, perhaps, will make an objection to one of the former arguments. "If men, from *superiority* of their nature, cannot be considered, like lands, goods, or houses, among possessions, so neither can cattle: for being endued with life, motion, and sensibility, they are evidently *superiour* to these." But this objection will receive its answer from those observations which have been already made; and will discover the true reason, why cattle are justly to be estimated as property. For first, the right to empire over brutes, is *natural*, and not *adventitious*, like the right to empire over men. There are, secondly, many and evident signs of the *inferiority* of their nature; and thirdly, their liberty can be bought and sold, because, being void of reason, they cannot be *accountable* for their actions.

We might stop here for a considerable time, and deduce many valuable lessons from the remarks that have been made, but that such a circumstance might be considered as a digression. There is one, however, which, as it is so intimately connected with the subject, we cannot but deduce. We are taught to treat men in a different manner from brutes, because they are so manifestly superiour in their nature; we are taught to treat brutes in a different manner from stones, for the same reason; and thus, by giving to every created thing its due respect, to answer the views of Providence, which did not create a variety of natures without a purpose or design.

But if these things are so, how evidently against reason, nature, and every thing human and divine, must they act, who not only force men into *slavery*, against their own *consent*; but treat them altogether as *brutes*, and make the *natural liberty* of man an article of publick commerce! and by what arguments can they possibly defend that commerce, which cannot be carried on, in any single instance, without a flagrant violation of the laws of nature and of God?

Chapter 5

That we may the more accurately examine the arguments that are advanced on this occasion, it will be proper to divide the *commerce* into two parts; first, as it relates to those who *sell*, and secondly, as it relates to those who *purchase*, the *human species* into slavery. To the former part of which, having given every previous and necessary information in the history of servitude, we shall immediately proceed.

Let us inquire first, by what particular right the *liberties* of the harmless people are invaded by the *prince*. "By the *right of empire*," it will be answered; "because he possesses dominion and power by their own approbation and consent." But subjects, though under the dominion, are not the *property*, of the prince. They cannot be considered as his *possessions*. Their *natures* are both the same; they are both born in the same manner; are subject to the same disorders; must apply to the same remedies for a cure; are equally partakers of the grave: an *incidental* distinction accompanies them through life, and this-is all.

We may add to this, that though the prince possesses dominion and power, by the consent and approbation of his subjects, he possesses it only for the most *salutary* ends. He may tyrannize, if he can: he may alter the *form* of his government: he cannot, however, alter its *nature* and *end*. These will be immutably the same, though the whole system of its administration should be changed; and he will be still bound to *defend* the lives and properties of his subjects, and to make them *happy*.

Does he defend those therefore, whom he invades at discretion with the sword? Does he protect the property of those, whose houses and effects he consigns at discretion to the flames? Does he make those happy, whom he seizes, as they are trying to escape the general devastation, and compels with their wives and families to a wretched *servitude?* He acts surely, as if the use of empire consisted in violence and oppression; as if he, that was most exalted, ought, of necessity, to be most unjust. Here then the voice of *nature* and *justice* is against him. He breaks that law of *nature*, which ordains, "that no just man shall be given into slavery, against his own *consent*:" he violates the first law of *justice*, as established among men, "that no person shall do harm to another without a previous and sufficient *provocation*;" and he violates also the sacred condition of *empire*, made with his ancestors, and necessarily understood in every species of government, "that, the power of the multitude being given up to the wisdom and justice of the prince, they may experience, in return, the most effectual protection from injury, the highest advantages of society, the greatest possible *happiness*."

But if kings then, to whom their own people have granted dominion and power, are unable to invade the liberties of their harmless subjects, without the highest *injustice*; how can those private persons be justified, who treacherously lie in wait for their fellow-creatures, and sell them into slavery? What arguments can they possibly bring in their defence? What treaty of empire can they produce, by which their innocent victims ever resigned to them the least portion of their *liberty*? In vain will they plead the *antiquity* of the custom: in vain will the *honourable* light, in which *piracy* was considered in the ages of barbarism, afford them an excuse. Impious and abandoned men! ye invade the liberties of those, who, (with respect to your impious selves) are in a state of *nature*, in a state of original *dissociation*, perfectly *independent*, perfectly *free*.

It appears then, that the two orders of slaves, which have been mentioned in the history of the African servitude, "of those who are publickly seized by virtue of the authority of their prince; and of those, who are privately kidnapped by individuals," are collected by means of violence and oppression; by means, repugnant to *nature*, the principles of *government*, and the common notions of *equity*, as established among men.

Chapter 6

\We come now to the third order of *involuntary* slaves, "to convicts." The only argument that the sellers advance here, is this, "that they have been found guilty of offences, and that the punishment is just." But before the equity of the sentence can be allowed two questions must be decided, whether the punishment is *proportioned* to the offence, and what is its particular *object* and *end*?

To decide the first, we may previously observe, that the African servitude comprehends *banishment*, a *deprivation* of *liberty*, and many *corporal* sufferings.

On *banishment*, the following observations will suffice. Mankind have their *local* attachments. They have a particular regard for the spot, in which they were born and nurtured. Here it was, that they first drew their infant-breath: here, that they were cherished and supported: here, that they passed those scenes of childhood, which, free from care and anxiety, are the happiest in the life of man; scenes, which accompany them through life; which throw themselves frequently into their thoughts, and produce the most agreeable sensations. These then are weighty considerations; and how great this regard is, may be evidenced from our own feelings; from the testimony of some, who, when remote from their country, and, in the hour of danger and distress, have found their thoughts unusually directed, by some impulse or other, to their native spot; and from the example of others, who, having braved the storms and adversities of life, either repair to it for the remainder of their days, or desire even to be conveyed to it, when existence is no more.

But separately from these their *local*, they have also their *personal* attachments; their regard for particular men. There are ties of blood; there are ties of friendship. In the former case, they must of necessity be attached: the constitution of their nature demands it. In the latter, it is impossible to be otherwise, since friendship is founded on an harmony of temper, on a concordance of sentiments and manners, on habits of confidence, and a mutual exchange of favours.

We may now mention, as perfectly distinct both from their *local* and *personal*, the *national* attachments of mankind, their regard for the whole body of the people, among whom they were born and educated. This regard is particularly conspicuous in the conduct of such, as, being thus *nationally* connected, reside in foreign parts. How anxiously do they meet together! how much do they enjoy the fight of others of their countrymen, whom fortune places in their way! what an eagerness do they show to serve them, though not born on the same particular spot, though not connected by consanguinity or friendship, though unknown to them before! Neither is this affection wonderful, since they are creatures of the same education; of the same principles; of the same manners and habits; cast, as it were, in the same mould; and marked with the same impression.

If men therefore are thus separately attached to the several objects described, it is evident that a separate exclusion from either must afford them considerable pain. What then must be their sufferings, to be forced for ever from their country, which includes them all? Which contains the *spot*, in which they were born and nurtured; which contains their *relations* and *friends*; which contains the whole body of the *people*, among whom they were bred and educated. In these sufferings, which arise to men, both in bidding, and in having bid, adieu to all that they esteem as dear and valuable, *banishment* consists in part; and we may agree therefore with the ancients, without adding other melancholy circumstances to the account, that it is no inconsiderable punishment of itself.

With respect to the *loss* of *liberty*, which is the second consideration in the punishment, it is evident that men bear nothing worse; that there is nothing, that they lay more at heart; and that they have shewn, by many and memorable instances, that even death is to be preferred. How many could be named here, who, having suffered the *loss* of *liberty*, have put a period to their existence! How many, that have willingly undergone the hazard of their lives to destroy a tyrant! How many, that have even gloried to perish in the attempt! How many bloody and publick wars have been undertaken (not to mention the numerous *servile* insurrections, with which history is stained) for the cause of *freedom*!

But if nothing is dearer than *liberty* to men, with which, the barren rock is able to afford its joys, and without which, the glorious fun shines upon them but in vain, and all the sweets and delicacies of life are tasteless and unenjoyed; what punishment can be more severe than the loss of so great a blessing? But if to this *deprivation* of *liberty*, we add the agonizing pangs of *banishment*; and if to the complicated stings of both, we add the incessant *stripes, wounds*, and *miseries*, which are undergone by those, who are sold into this horrid *servitude*; what crime can we possibly imagine to be so enormous, as to be worthy of so great a punishment?

How contrary then to reason, justice, and nature, must those act, who apply this, the severest of human punishments, to the most insignificant offence! yet such is the custom with the Africans: for, from the time, in which the Europeans first intoxicated the African princes with their foreign draughts, no crime has been committed, no shadow of a crime devised, that has not immediately been punished with *servitude*.

But for what purpose is the punishment applied? Is it applied to amend the manners of the criminal, and thus render him a better subject? No, for if you banish him, he can no longer be a subject, and you can no longer therefore be solicitous for his morals. Add to this, that if you banish him to a place, where he is to experience the hardships of want and hunger (so powerfully does hunger compel men to the perpetration of crimes) you force him rather to corrupt, than amend his manners, and to be wicked, when he might otherwise be just.

Is it applied then, that others may be deterred from the same proceedings, and that crimes may become less frequent? No, but that *avarice* may be gratified; that the prince may experience the emoluments of the sale: for, horrid and melancholy thought! the more crimes his subjects commit, the richer is he made; the more *abandoned* the subject, the *happier* is the prince!

Neither can we allow that the punishment thus applied, tends in any degree to answer *publick happiness*; for if men can be sentenced to slavery, right or wrong; if shadows can be turned into substances, and virtues into crimes; it is evident that none can be happy, because none can be secure.

But if the punishment is infinitely greater than the offence, (which has been shewn before) and if it is inflicted, neither to amend the criminal, nor to deter others from the same proceedings, nor to advance, in any degree, the happiness of the publick, it is scarce necessary to observe, that it is totally unjust, since it is repugnant to *reason*, the dictates of *nature*, and the very principles of *government*.

Chapter 7

We come now to the fourth and last order of slaves, to *prisoners of war*. As the *sellers* lay a particular stress on this order of men, and infer much, from its *antiquity*, in support of the justice of their cause, we shall examine the principle, on which it subsisted among the ancients. But as this principle was the same among all nations, and as a citation from many of their histories would not be less tedious than unnecessary, we shall select the example of the Romans for the consideration of the case.

The law, by which prisoners of war were said to be sentenced to servitude, was the *law of nations*.[43] It was so called from the universal concurrence of nations in the custom. It had two points in view, the *persons* of the *captured*, and their *effects*; both of which it immediately sentenced, without any of the usual forms of law, to be the property of the *captors*.

The principle, on which the law was established, was the *right of capture*. When any of the contending parties had overcome their opponents, and were about to destroy them, the right was considered to commence; a right, which the victors conceived themselves to have, to recall their swords, and, from the consideration of having saved the lives of the vanquished, when they could have taken them by the laws of war, to commute *blood* for *service*. Hence the Roman lawyer, Pomponius, deduces the etymology of *slave* in the Roman language. "They were called *servi*,[44] says he from the following circumstance. It was usual with our commanders to take them prisoners, and sell them: now this circumstance implies, that they must have been previously *preserved*, and hence the name." Such then was the *right of capture*. It was a right, which the circumstance of *taking* the vanquished, that is, of *preserving* them alive, gave the conquerors to their persons. By this right, as always including the idea of a previous preservation from death, the vanquished were said *to be slaves*;[45] and, "as all slaves," says Justinian, "are themselves in the power of others, and of course can have nothing of their own, so their effects followed the condition of their persons, and became the property of the captors."

To examine this right, by which the vanquished were said to be slaves, we shall use the words of a celebrated Roman author, and apply them to the present case.[46] "If it is lawful," says he, "to deprive a man of his life, it is certainly not inconsistent with nature to rob him;" to rob him of his liberty. We admit the conclusion to be just, if the supposition be the same: we allow, if men have a right to commit that, which is considered as a greater crime, that they have a right, at the same instant, to commit that, which is considered as a less. But what shall we say to the *hypothesis*? We deny it to be true. The voice of nature is against it. It is not lawful to kill, but on *necessity*. Had there been a necessity, where had the wretched captive survived to be broken with chains and servitude? The very act of saving his life is an argument to prove, that no such necessity existed. The *conclusion* is therefore false. The captors had no right to the *lives* of the captured, and of course none to their *liberty*: they had no right to their *blood*, and of course none to their *service*. Their right therefore had no foundation in justice. It was founded on a principle, contrary to the law of nature, and of course contrary to that law, which people, under different governments, are bound to observe to one another.

It is scarce necessary to observe, as a farther testimony of the injustice of the measure, that the Europeans, after the introduction of Christianity, exploded this principle of the ancients, as frivolous and false; that they spared the lives of the vanquished, not from the sordid motives of *avarice*, but from a conscientiousness, that homicide could only be justified by *necessity*; that they introduced an *exchange* of prisoners, and, by many and wise regulations, deprived war of many of its former horrours.

But the advocates for slavery, unable to defend themselves against these arguments, have fled to other resources, and, ignorant of history, have denied that the *right of capture* was the true principle, on which slavery subsisted among the ancients. They reason thus. "The learned Grotius, and others, have considered slavery as the just consequence of a private war, (supposing the war to be just and the opponents in a state of nature), upon the principles of *reparation* and *punishment*. Now as the law of nature, which is the rule of conduct to individuals in such a situation, is applicable to members of a different community, there is reason to presume, that these principles were applied by the ancients to their prisoners of war; that their *effects* were confiscated by the right of *reparation*, and their *persons* by the right of *punishment*."-

But, such a presumption is false. The *right of capture* was the only argument, that the ancients adduced in their defence. Hence Polybius; "What must they, (the Mantinenses) suffer, to receive the punishment they deserve? Perhaps it will be said, *that they must be sold, when they are taken, with their wives and children into slavery*: But this is not to be considered as a punishment, since even those suffer it, by the laws of war, who have done nothing that is base." The truth is, that both the *offending* and the *offended* parties, whenever they were victorious, inflicted slavery alike. But if the *offending* party inflicted slavery on the persons of the vanquished, by what right did they inflict it? It must be answered from the presumption before-mentioned, "by the right of *reparation*, or of *punishment:*" an answer plainly absurd and contradictory, as it supposes the *aggressor* to have a *right*, which the *injured* only could possess.

Neither is the argument less fallacious than the presumption, in applying these principles, which in a *publick* war could belong to the *publick* only, to the persons of the *individuals* that were taken. This calls us again to the history of the ancients, and, as the rights of reparation and punishment could extend to those only, who had been injured, to select a particular instance for the consideration of the case.

As the Romans had been injured without a previous provocation by the conduct of Hannibal at Saguntum, we may take the treaty into consideration, which they made with the Carthaginians, when the latter, defeated at Zama, sued for peace. It consisted of three articles.[47] By the first, the Carthaginians were to be free, and to enjoy their own constitution and laws. By the second, they were to pay a considerable sum of money, as a reparation for the damages and expence of war: and, by the third, they were to deliver up their elephants and ships of war, and to be subject to various restrictions, as a punishment. With these terms they complied, and the war was finished.

Thus then did the Romans make that distinction between *private* and *publick* war, which was necessary to be made, and which the argument is fallacious in not supposing. The treasury of the vanquished was marked as the means of *reparation*; and as this treasury was supplied, in a great measure, by the imposition of taxes, and was, wholly, the property of the *publick*, so the *publick* made the reparation that was due. The *elephants* also, and *ships of war*, which were marked as the means of *punishment*, were *publick* property; and as they were considerable instruments of security and defence to their possessors, and of

57

annoyance to an enemy, so their loss, added to the restrictions of the treaty, operated as a great and *publick* punishment. But with respect to the Carthaginian prisoners, who had been taken in the war, they were retained in *servitude:* not upon the principles of *reparation* and *punishment*, because the Romans had already received, by their own confession in the treaty, a sufficient satisfaction: not upon these principles, because they were inapplicable to *individuals:* the legionary soldier in the service of the injured, who took his prisoner, was not the person, to whom the *injury had been done*, any more than the soldier in the service of the aggressors, who was taken, was the person, who had *committed the offence:* but they were retained in servitude by the *right of capture*; because, when both parties had sent their military into the field to determine the dispute, it was at the *private* choice of the legionary soldier before-mentioned, whether he would spare the life of his conquered opponent, when he was thought to be entitled to take it, if he had chosen, by the laws of war.

To produce more instances, as an illustration of the subject, or to go farther into the argument, would be to trespass upon the patience, as well as understanding of the reader. In *a state of nature*, where a man is supposed to commit an injury, and to be unconnected with the rest of the world, the act is *private*, and the right, which the injured acquires, can extend only to *himself:* but in *a state of society*, where any member or members of a particular community give offence to those of another, and they are patronized by the state, to which they belong, the case is altered; the act becomes immediately *publick*, and the *publick* alone are to experience the consequences of their injustice. For as no particular member of the community, if considered as an individual, is guilty, except the person, by whom the injury was done, it would be contrary to reason and justice, to apply the principles of *reparation* and *punishment*, which belong to the people as a collective body, to any individual of the community, who should happen to be taken. Now, as the principles of *reparation* and *punishment* are thus inapplicable to the prisoners, taken in a *publick* war, and as the *right of capture*, as we have shewn before, is insufficient to intitle the victors to the *service* of the vanquished, it is evident that *slavery* cannot justly exist at all, since there are no other maxims, on which it can be founded, even in the most equitable wars.

But if these things are so; if slavery cannot be defended even in the most *equitable* wars, what arguments will not be found against that servitude, which arises from those, that are *unjust?* Which arises from those African wars, that relate to the present subject? The African

58

princes, corrupted by the merchants of Europe, seek every opportunity of quarrelling with one another. Every spark is blown into a flame; and war is undertaken from no other consideration, than that *of procuring slaves:* while the Europeans, on the other hand, happy in the quarrels which they have thus excited, supply them with arms and ammunition for the accomplishment of their horrid purpose. Thus has Africa, for the space of two hundred years, been the scene of the most iniquitous and bloody wars; and thus have many thousands of men, in the most iniquitous manner, been sent into servitude.

Chapter 8

We shall beg leave, before we proceed to the arguments of the *purchasers*, to add the following observations to the substance of the three preceding chapters.

As the two orders of men, of those who are privately kidnapped by individuals, and of those who are publickly seized by virtue of the authority of their prince, compose together, at least,[48] nine tenths of the African slaves, they cannot contain, upon a moderate computation, less than ninety thousand men annually transported: an immense number, but easily to be credited, when we reflect that thousands are employed for the purpose of stealing the unwary, and that these diabolical practices are in force, so far has European *injustice* been spread, at the distance of a thousand miles from the factories on the coast. The *slave merchants*, among whom a quantity of European goods is previously divided, travel into the heart of the country to this amazing distance. Some of them attend the various markets, that are established through so large an extent of territory, to purchase the kidnapped people, whom the *slave-hunters* are continually bringing in; while the rest, subdividing their merchandize among the petty sovereigns with whom they deal, receive, by an immediate exertion of fraud and violence, the stipulated number.

Now, will any man assert, in opposition to the arguments before advanced, that out of this immense body of men, thus annually collected and transported, there is even *one*, over whom the original or subsequent seller can have any power or right? Whoever asserts this, in the first instance, must, contradict his own feelings, and must consider *himself* as a just object of prey, whenever any daring invader shall think it proper to attack *him*. And, in the second instance, the very idea which the African princes entertain of their villages, as *parks* or *reservoirs*, stocked only for their own convenience, and of their subjects, as *wild beasts*, whom they may pursue and take at pleasure, is so shocking, that it need only be mentioned, to be instantly reprobated by the reader.

The order of slaves, which is next to the former in respect to the number of people whom it contains, is that of prisoners of war. This order, if the former statement be true, is more inconsiderable than is generally imagined; but whoever reflects on the prodigious slaughter that is constantly made in every African skirmish, cannot be otherwise than of this opinion: he will find, that where *ten* are taken, he has every reason to presume that an *hundred* perish. In some of these skirmishes, though they have been begun for the express purpose of *procuring slaves*, the conquerors have suffered but few of the vanquished to escape the fury of the sword; and there have not been wanting instances, where they have been so incensed at the resistance they have found, that their spirit of vengeance has entirely got the better of their avarice, and they have murdered, in cool blood, every individual, without discrimination, either of age or sex.

The following[49] is an account of one of these skirmishes, as described by a person, who was witness to the scene. "I was sent, with several others, in a small sloop up the river Niger, to purchase slaves: we had some free negroes with us in the practice; and as the vessels are liable to frequent attacks from the negroes on one side of the river, or the Moors on the other, they are all armed. As we rode at anchor a long way up the river, we observed a large number of negroes in huts by the river's side, and for our own safety kept a wary eye on them. Early next morning we saw from our masthead a numerous body approaching, with apparently but little order, but in close array. They approached very fast, and fell furiously on the inhabitants of the town, who seemed to be quite *surprized*, but nevertheless, as soon as they could get together, fought stoutly. They had some fire-arms, but made very little use of them, as they came directly to close fighting with their spears, lances, and sabres. Many of the invaders were mounted on small horses; and both parties fought for about half an hour with the fiercest animosity, exerting much more courage and perseverance than I had ever before been witness to amongst them. The women and children of the town clustered together to the water's edge, running shrieking up and down with terrour, waiting the event of the combat, till their party gave way and took to the water, to endeavour to swim over to the Barbary side. They were closely pursued even into the river by the victors, who, though they came for the purpose of *getting slaves*, gave no quarter, *their cruelty even prevailing over their avarice*. They made no prisoners, but put all to the sword without mercy.

Horrible indeed was the carnage of the vanquished on this occasion, and as we were within two or three hundred yards of them, their cries and shrieks affected us extremely. We had got up our anchor at the beginning of the fray, and now stood close in to the spot, where the victors having followed the vanquished into the water, were continually dragging out and murdering those, whom by reason of their wounds they easily overtook. The very children, whom they took in great numbers, did not escape the massacre. Enraged at their barbarity, we fired our guns loaden with grape shot, and a volley of small arms among them, which effectually checked their ardour, and obliged them to retire to a distance from the shore; from whence a few round cannon shot soon removed them into the woods. The whole river was black over with the heads of the fugitives, who were swimming for their lives. These poor wretches, fearing *us* as much as their conquerors, dived when we fired, and cried most lamentably for mercy. Having now effectually favoured their retreat, we stood backwards and forwards, and took up several that were wounded and tired. All whose wounds had disabled them from swimming, were either butchered or drowned, before we got up to them. With a justice and generosity, *never I believe before heard of among slavers*, we gave those their liberty whom we had taken up, setting them on shore on the Barbary side, among the poor residue of their companions, who had survived the slaughter of the morning."

We shall make but two remarks on this horrid instance of African cruelty. It adds, first, a considerable weight to the statements that have been made; and confirms, secondly, the conclusions that were drawn in the preceding chapter. For if we even allow the right of capture to be just, and the principles of reparation and punishment to be applicable to the individuals of a community, yet would the former be unjust, and the latter inapplicable, in the present case. Every African war is a robbery; and we may add, to our former expression, when we said, "that thus have many thousands of men, in the most iniquitous manner, been sent into servitude," that we believe there are few of this order, who are not as much the examples of injustice, as the people that have been kidnapped; and who do not additionally convey, when we consider them as prisoners of war, an idea of the most complicated scene of murder.

The order of *convicts*, as it exists almost solely among those princes, whose dominions are contiguous to the European factories, is from this circumstance so inconsiderable, when compared with either of the preceding, that we should not have mentioned it again, but that we were unwilling to omit any additional argument that occurred against it.

It has been shewn already, that the punishment of slavery is inflicted from no other motive, than that of gratifying the *avarice* of the prince, a confederation so detestable, as to be sufficient of itself to prove it to be unjust; and that it is so disproportionate, from its *nature*, to the offence, as to afford an additional proof of its injustice. We shall add now, as a second argument, its disproportion from its *continuance:* and we shall derive a third from the consideration, that, in civil society, every violation of the laws of the community is an offence against the *state*.[50]

Let us suppose then an African prince, disdaining for once the idea of emolument: let us suppose him for once inflamed with the love of his country, and resolving to punish from this principle alone, "that by exhibiting an example of terrour, he may preserve that *happiness of the publick*, which he is bound to secure and defend by the very nature of his contract; or, in other words, that he may answer the end of government." If actuated then by this principle, he should adjudge slavery to an offender, as a just punishment for his offence, for whose benefit must the convict labour? If it be answered, "for the benefit of the state," we allow that the punishment, in whatever light it is considered, will be found to be equitable: but if it be answered, "for the benefit of any *individual whom he pleases to appoint*," we deny it to be just. The state[51] alone is considered to have been injured, and as *injuries cannot possibly be transferred*, the state alone can justly receive the advantages of his labour. But if the African prince, when he thus condemns him to labour for the benefit of an *unoffended individual*, should at the same time sentence him to become his *property*; that is, if he should make the person and life of the convict at the absolute disposal of him, for whom he has sentenced him to labour; it is evident that, in addition to his former injustice, he is usurping a power, which no ruler or rulers of a state can possess, and which the great Creator of the universe never yet gave to any order whatever of created beings.

That this reasoning is true, and that civilized nations have considered it as such, will be best testified by their practice. We may appeal here to that *slavery*, which is now adjudged to delinquents, as a punishment, among many of the states of Europe. These delinquents are sentenced to labour at the *oar*, to work in *mines*, and on *fortifications*, to cut and clear *rivers*, to make and repair *roads*, and to perform other works of national utility. They are employed, in short, in the *publick* work; because, as the crimes they have committed are considered to have been crimes against the publick, no individual can justly receive the emoluments of their labour; and they are neither *sold*, nor made capable of being *transferred*, because no government whatsoever is invested with such a power.

Thus then may that slavery, in which only the idea of *labour* is included, be perfectly equitable, and the delinquent will always receive his punishment as a man; whereas in that, which additionally includes the idea of *property*, and to undergo which, the delinquent must previously change his nature, and become a *brute*; there is an inconsistency, which no arguments can reconcile, and a contradiction to every principle of nature, which a man need only to appeal to his own feelings immediately to evince. And we will venture to assert, from the united observations that have been made upon the subject, in opposition to any arguments that may be advanced, that there is scarcely one of those, who are called African convicts, on whom the prince has a right to inflict a punishment at all; and that there is no one whatever, whom he has a power of sentencing to labour for the benefit of an unoffended individual, and much less whom he has a right to sell.

Having now fully examined the arguments of the *sellers*,[52] and having made such additional remarks as were necessary, we have only to add, that we cannot sufficiently express our detestation at their conduct. Were the reader coolly to reflect upon the case of but *one* of the unfortunate men, who are annually the victims of *avarice*, and consider his situation in life, as a father, an husband, or a friend, we are sure, that even on such a partial reflection, he must experience considerable pain. What then must be his feelings, when he is told, that, since the slave-trade began, *nine millions* [53] of men have been torn from their dearest connections, and sold into slavery. If at this recital his indignation should arise, let him consider it as the genuine production of nature; that she recoiled at the horrid thought, and that she applied instantly a torch to his breast to kindle his resentment; and if, during his indignation, she should awaken the sigh of sympathy, or seduce the tear of commiseration from his eye, let him consider each as an additional argument against the iniquity of the *sellers*.

Chapter 9

It remains only now to examine by what arguments those, who *receive* or *purchase* their fellow-creatures into slavery, defend the *commerce*. Their first plea is, "that they receive those with propriety, who are convicted of crimes, because they are delivered into their hands by *their own magistrates*." But what is this to you *receivers*? Have the unfortunate *convicts* been guilty of injury to *you*? Have they broken *your* treaties? Have they plundered *your* ships? Have they carried *your* wives and children into slavery, that *you* should thus retaliate? Have they offended *you* even by word or gesture?

But if the African convicts are innocent with respect to you; if you have not even the shadow of a claim upon their persons; by what right do you receive them? "By the laws of the Africans," you will say; "by which it is positively allowed."-But can *laws* alter the nature of vice? They may give it a sanction perhaps: it will still be immutably the same, and, though dressed in the outward habiliments of *honour*, will still be *intrinsically base*.

But alas! you do not only attempt to defend yourselves by these arguments, but even dare to give your actions the appearance of lenity, and assume *merit* from your *baseness*! and how first ought you particularly to blush, when you assert, "that prisoners of war are only purchased from the hands of their conquerors, *to deliver them from death*." Ridiculous defence! can the most credulous believe it? You entice the Africans to war; you foment their quarrels; you supply them with arms and ammunition, and all-from the *motives of benevolence*. Does a man set fire to an house, for the purpose of rescuing the inhabitants from the flames? But if they are only purchased, to *deliver them from death*; why, when they are delivered into your hands, as protectors, do you torture them with hunger? Why do you kill them with fatigue? Why does the whip deform their bodies, or the knife their limbs? Why do you sentence them to death? to a death, infinitely more excruciating than that from which you so kindly saved them? What answer do you make to this? for if you had not humanely preserved them from the hands of their conquerors, a quick death perhaps, and that in the space of a moment, had freed them from their pain: but on account of your *favour* and *benevolence*, it is known, that they have lingered years in pain and agony, and have been sentenced, at last, to a dreadful death for the most insignificant offence.

Neither can we allow the other argument to be true, on which you found your merit; "that you take them from their country for their own convenience; because Africa, scorched with incessant heat, and subject to the most violent rains and tempests, is unwholesome, and unfit to be inhabited." Preposterous men! do you thus judge from your own feelings? Do you thus judge from your own constitution and frame? But if you suppose that the Africans are incapable of enduring their own climate, because you cannot endure it yourselves; why do you receive them into slavery? Why do you not measure them here by the same standard? For if you are unable to bear hunger and thirst, chains and imprisonment, wounds and torture, why do you not suppose them incapable of enduring the same treatment? Thus then is your argument turned against yourselves. But consider the answer which the Scythians gave the Ægyptians, when they contended about the antiquity of their original,[54] "That nature, when she first distinguished countries by different degrees of heat and cold, tempered the bodies of animals, at the same instant, to endure the different situations: that as the climate of Scythia was severer than that of Ægypt, so were the bodies of the Scythians harder, and as capable of enduring the severity of their atmosphere, as the Ægyptians the temperateness of their own."

But you may say perhaps, that, though they are capable of enduring their own climate, yet their situation is frequently uncomfortable, and even wretched: that Africa is infested with locusts, and insects of various kinds; that they settle in swarms upon the trees, destroy the verdure, consume the fruit, and deprive the inhabitants of their food. But the same answer may be applied as before; "that the same kind Providence, who tempered the body of the animal, tempered also the body of the tree; that he gave it a quality to recover the bite of the locust, which he sent; and to reassume, in a short interval of time, its former glory." And that such is the case experience has shewn: for the very trees that have been infested, and stripped of their bloom and verdure, so surprizingly quick is vegetation, appear in a few days, as if an insect had been utterly unknown.

We may add to these observations, from the testimony of those who have written the History of Africa from their own inspection, that no country is more luxurious in prospects, none more fruitful, none more rich in herds and flocks, and none, where the comforts of life, can be gained with so little trouble.

But you say again, as a confirmation of these your former arguments, (by which you would have it understood, that the Africans themselves are sensible of the goodness of your intentions) "that they do not appear to go with you against their will." Impudent and base assertion! Why then do you load them with chains? Why keep you your daily and nightly watches? But alas, as a farther, though a more melancholy proof, of the falsehood of your assertions, how many, when on board your ships, have put a period to their existence? How many have leaped into the sea? How many have pined to death, that, even at the expence of their lives, they might fly from your *benevolence*?

Do you call them obstinate then, because they refuse your favours? Do you call them ungrateful, because they make you this return? How much rather ought you receivers to blush! How much rather ought you receivers to be considered as abandoned and execrable; who, when you usurp the dominion over those, who are as free and independent as yourselves, break the first law of justice, which ordains, "that no person shall do harm to another, without a previous provocation;" who offend against the dictates of nature, which commands, "that no just man shall be given or received into slavery against his own consent;" and who violate the very laws of the empire that you assume, by consigning your subjects to misery.

Now, as a famous Heathen philosopher observes, from whose mouth you shall be convicted,[55] "there is a considerable difference, whether an injury is done, during any perturbation of mind, which is generally short and momentary; or whether it is done with any previous meditation and design; for, those crimes, which proceed from any sudden commotion of the mind, are less than those, which are studied and prepared," how great and enormous are your crimes to be considered, who plan your African voyages at a time, when your reason is found, and your senses are awake; who coolly and deliberately equip your vessels; and who spend years, and even lives, in the traffick of *human liberty*.

But if the arguments of those, who *sell* or *deliver* men into slavery, (as we have shewn before) and of those, who *receive* or *purchase* them, (as we have now shewn) are wholly false; it is evident that this *commerce*, is not only beyond the possibility of defence, but is justly to be accounted wicked, and justly impious, since it is contrary to the principles of *law* and *government*, the dictates of *reason*, the common maxims of *equity*, the laws of *nature*, the admonitions of *conscience*, and, in short, the whole doctrine of *natural religion*.

Part 3:
The Slavery of the Africans in the European Colonies

Chapter 1

Having confined ourselves wholly, in the second part of this Essay, to the consideration of the *commerce*, we shall now proceed to the consideration of the *slavery* that is founded upon it. As this slavery will be conspicuous in the *treatment*, which the unfortunate Africans uniformly undergo, when they are put into the hands of the *receivers*, we shall describe the manner in which they are accustomed to be used from this period.

To place this in the clearest, and most conspicuous point of view, we shall throw a considerable part of our information on this head into the form of a narrative: we shall suppose ourselves, in short, on the continent of Africa, and relate a scene, which, from its agreement with unquestionable facts, might not unreasonably be presumed to have been presented to our view, had we been really there.

And first, let us turn our eyes to the cloud of dust that is before us. It seems to advance rapidly, and, accompanied with dismal shrieks and yellings, to make the very air, that is above it, tremble as it rolls along. What can possibly be the cause? Let us inquire of that melancholy African, who seems to walk dejected near the shore; whose eyes are stedfastly fixed on the approaching object, and whose heart, if we can judge from the appearance of his countenance, must be greatly agitated.

"Alas!" says the unhappy African, "the cloud that you see approaching, is a train of wretched slaves. They are going to the ships behind you. They are destined for the English colonies, and, if you will stay here but for a little time, you will see them pass. They were last night drawn up upon the plain which you see before you, where they were branded upon the breast with an *hot iron*; and when they had undergone the whole of the treatment which is customary on these occasions, and which I am informed that you Englishmen at home use to the *cattle* which you buy, they were returned to their prison. As I have some dealings with the members of the factory which you see at a little distance, (though thanks to the Great Spirit, I never dealt in the *liberty* of my fellow creatures) I gained admittance there. I learned the history of some of the unfortunate people, whom I saw confined, and will explain to you, if my eye should catch them as they pass, the real causes of their servitude."

Scarcely were these words spoken, when they came distinctly into sight. They appeared to advance in a long column, but in a very irregular manner. There were three only in the front, and these were chained together. The rest that followed seemed to be chained by pairs, but by pressing forward, to avoid the lash of the drivers, the breadth of the column began to be greatly extended, and ten or more were observed abreast.

While we were making these remarks, the intelligent African thus resumed his discourse. "The first three whom you observe, at the head of the train, to be chained together, are prisoners of war. As soon as the ships that are behind you arrived, the news was dispatched into the inland country; when one of the petty kings immediately assembled his subjects, and attacked a neighbouring tribe. The wretched people, though they were surprized, made a formidable resistance, as they resolved, almost all of them, rather to lose their lives, than survive their liberty. The person whom you see in the middle, is the father of the two young men, who are chained to him on each side. His wife and two of his children were killed in the attack, and his father being wounded, and, on account of his age, *incapable of servitude*, was left bleeding on the spot where this transaction happened."

"With respect to those who are now passing us, and are immediately behind the former, I can give you no other intelligence, than that some of them, to about the number of thirty, were taken in the same skirmish. Their tribe was said to have been numerous before the attack; these however are *all that are left alive*. But with respect to the unhappy man, who is now opposite to us, and whom you may distinguish, as he is now looking back and wringing his hands in despair, I can inform you with more precision. He is an unfortunate convict. He lived only about five days journey from the factory. He went out with his king to hunt, and was one of his train; but, through too great an anxiety to afford his royal master diversion, he roused the game from the covert rather sooner than was expected. The king, exasperated at this circumstance, immediately sentenced him to slavery. His wife and children, fearing lest the tyrant should extend the punishment to themselves, *which is not unusual*, fled directly to the woods, where they were all devoured."

"The people, whom you see close behind the unhappy convict, form a numerous body, and reach a considerable way. They speak a language, which no person in this part of Africa can understand, and their features, as you perceive, are so different from those of the rest, that they almost appear a distinct race of men. From this circumstance I recollect them. They are the subjects of a very distant prince, who agreed with the *slave merchants, for a quantity of spirituous liquors,* to furnish him with a stipulated number of slaves. He accordingly surrounded, and set fire to one of his own villages in the night, and seized these people, who were unfortunately the inhabitants, as they were escaping from the flames. I first saw them as the merchants were driving them in, about two days ago. They came in a large body, and were tied together at the neck with leather thongs, which permitted them to walk at the distance of about a yard from one another. Many of them were loaden with elephants teeth, which had been purchased at the same time. All of them had bags, made of skin, upon their shoulders; for as they were to travel, in their way from the great mountains, through barren sands and inhospitable woods for many days together, they were obliged to carry water and provisions with them. Notwithstanding this, many of them perished, some by hunger, but the greatest number by fatigue, as the place from whence they came, is at such an amazing distance from this, and the obstacles, from the nature of the country, so great, that the journey could scarcely be completed in seven moons."

When this relation was finished, and we had been looking stedfastly for some time on the croud that was going by, we lost sight of that peculiarity of feature, which we had before remarked. We then discovered that the inhabitants of the depopulated village had all of them passed us, and that the part of the train, to which we were now opposite, was a numerous body of kidnapped people. Here we indulged our imagination. We thought we beheld in one of them a father, in another an husband, and in another a son, each of whom was forced from his various and tender connections, and without even the opportunity of bidding them adieu. While we were engaged in these and other melancholy reflections, the whole body of slaves had entirely passed us. We turned almost insensibly to look at them again, when we discovered an unhappy man at the end of the train, who could scarcely keep pace with the rest. His feet seemed to have suffered much from long and constant travelling, for he was limping painfully along.

"This man," resumes the African. "has travelled a considerable way. He lived at a great distance from hence, and had a large family, for whom he was daily to provide. As he went out one night to a neighbouring spring, to procure water for his thirsty children, he was kidnapped by two *slave hunters*, who sold him in the morning to some country merchants for a *bar of iron*. These drove him with other slaves, procured almost in the same manner, to the nearest market, where the English merchants, to whom the train that has just now passed us belongs, purchased him and two others, by means of their travelling agents, for a *pistol*. His wife and children have been long waiting for his return. But he is gone for ever from their sight: and they must be now disconsolate, as they must be certain by his delay, that he has fallen into the hands of the *Christians*".

"And now, as I have mentioned the name of *Christians*, a name, by which the Europeans distinguish themselves from us, I could wish to be informed of the meaning which such an appellation may convey. They consider themselves as *men*, but us unfortunate Africans, whom they term *Heathens*, as the *beasts* that serve us. But ah! how different is the fact! What is *Christianity*, but a system of *murder* and *oppression*? The cries and yells of the unfortunate people, who are now soon to embark for the regions of servitude, have already pierced my heart. Have you not heard me sigh, while we have been talking? Do you not see the tears that now trickle down my cheeks? and yet these hardened *Christians* are unable to be moved at all: nay, they will scourge them amidst their groans, and even smile, while they are torturing them to death. Happy, happy Heathenism! which can detest the vices of Christianity, and feel for the distresses of mankind."

"But" we reply, "You are totally mistaken: *Christianity* is the most perfect and lovely of moral systems. It blesses even the hand of persecution itself, and returns good for evil. But the people against whom you so justly declaim; are not *Christians*. They are *infidels*. They are *monsters*. They are out of the common course of nature. Their countrymen at home are generous and brave. They support the sick, the lame, and the blind. They fly to the succour of the distressed. They have noble and stately buildings for the sole purpose of benevolence. They are in short, of all nations, the most remarkable for humanity and justice."

"But why then," replies the honest African, "do they suffer this? Why is Africa a scene of blood and desolation? Why are her children wrested from her, to administer to the luxuries and greatness of those whom they never offended? And why are these dismal cries in vain?"

"Alas!" we reply again, "can the cries and groans, with which the air now trembles, be heard across this extensive continent? Can the southern winds convey them to the ear of Britain? If they could reach the generous Englishman at home, they would pierce his heart, as they have already pierced your own. He would sympathize with you in your distress. He would be enraged at the conduct of his countrymen, and resist their tyranny."-

But here a shriek unusually loud, accompanied with a dreadful rattling of chains, interrupted the discourse. The wretched Africans were just about to embark: they had turned their face to their country, as if to take a last adieu, and, with arms uplifted to the sky, were making the very atmosphere resound with their prayers and imprecations.

Chapter 2

The foregoing scene, though it may be said to be imaginary, is strictly consistent with fact. It is a scene, to which the reader himself may have been witness, if he has ever visited the place, where it is supposed to lie; as no circumstance whatever has been inserted in it, for which the fullest and most undeniable evidence cannot be produced. We shall proceed now to describe, in general terms, the treatment which the wretched Africans undergo, from the time of their embarkation.

When the African slaves, who are collected from various quarters, for the purposes of sale, are delivered over to the *receivers*, they are conducted in the manner above described to the ships. Their situation on board is beyond all description: for here they are crouded, hundreds of them together, into such a small compass, as would scarcely be thought sufficient to accommodate twenty, if considered as *free men*. This confinement soon produces an effect, that may be easily imagined. It generates a pestilential air, which, co-operating with, bad provisions, occasions such a sickness and mortality among them, that not less than *twenty thousand*[56] are generally taken off in every yearly transportation.

Thus confined in a pestilential prison, and almost entirely excluded from the chearful face of day, it remains for the sickly survivors to linger out a miserable existence, till the voyage is finished. But are no farther evils to be expected in the interim particularly if we add to their already wretched situation the indignities that are daily offered them, and the regret which they must constantly feel, at being for ever forced from their connexions? These evils are but too apparent. Some of them have resolved, and, notwithstanding the threats of the *receivers*, have carried their resolves into execution, to starve themselves to death. Others, when they have been brought upon deck for air, if the least opportunity has offered, have leaped into the sea, and terminated their miseries at once. Others, in a fit of despair, have attempted to rise, and regain their liberty. But here what a scene of barbarity has constantly ensued. Some of them have been instantly killed upon the spot; some have been taken from the hold, have been bruised and mutilated in the most barbarous and shocking manner, and have been returned bleeding to their companions, as a sad example of resistance; while others, tied to the ropes of the ship, and mangled alternately with the whip and knife, have been left in that horrid situation, till they have expired.

But this is not the only inhuman treatment which they are frequently obliged to undergo; for if there should be any necessity, from tempestuous weather, for lightening the ship; or if it should be presumed on the voyage, that the provisions will fall short before the port can be made, they are, many of them, thrown into the sea, without any compunction of mind on the part of the *receivers*, and without any other regret for their loss, than that which *avarice* inspires. Wretched survivors! what must be their feelings at such a sight! how must they tremble to think of that servitude which is approaching, when the very *dogs* of the *receivers* have been retained on board, and preferred to their unoffending countrymen. But indeed so lightly are these unhappy people esteemed, that their lives have been even taken away upon speculation: there has been an instance, within the last five years, of *one hundred and thirty two* of them being thrown into the sea, because it was supposed that, by this *trick*, their value could be recovered from the insurers.[57]

But if the ship should arrive safe at its destined port, a circumstance which does not always happen, (for some have been blown up, and many lost) the wretched Africans do not find an alleviation of their sorrow. Here they are again exposed to sale. Here they are again subjected to the inspection of other brutal *receivers*, who examine and treat them with an inhumanity, at which even avarice should blush. To this mortifying circumstance is added another, that they are picked out, as the purchaser pleases, without any consideration whether the wife is separated from her husband, or the mother from her son: and if these cruel instances of separation should happen; if relations, when they find themselves about to be parted, should cling together; or if filial, conjugal, or parental affection, should detain them but a moment longer in each other's arms, than these *second receivers* should think sufficient, the lash instantly severs them from their embraces.

We cannot close our account of the treatment, which the wretched Africans undergo while in the hands of the *first receivers*, without mentioning an instance of wanton, barbarity, which happened some time ago; particularly as it may be inserted with propriety in the present place, and may give the reader a better idea of the cruelties, to which they are continually exposed, than any that he may have yet conceived. To avoid making a mistake, we shall take the liberty that has been allowed us, and transcribe it from a little manuscript account, with which we have been favoured by a person of the strictest integrity, and who was at that time in the place where the transaction happened.[58] "Not long after," says he, (continuing his account) "the perpetrator of a cruel murder, committed in open day light, in the most publick part of a town, which was the seat of government, escaped every other notice than the curses of a few of the more humane witnesses of his barbarity. An officer of a Guinea ship, who had the care of a number of new slaves, and was returning from the *sale-yard* to the vessel with such as remained unsold; observed a stout fellow among them rather slow in his motions, which he therefore quickened with his rattan. The slave soon afterwards fell down, and was raised by the same application. Moving forwards a few yards, he fell down again; and this being taken as a proof of his sullen perverse spirit, the enraged officer furiously repeated his blows, till he expired at his feet. The brute coolly ordered some of the surviving slaves to carry the dead body to the water's side, where, without any ceremony or delay, being thrown into the sea, the tragedy was supposed to have been immediately finished by the not more inhuman sharks, with which the harbour then abounded. These voracious fish were supposed to have followed the vessels from the coast of Africa, in which ten thousand slaves were imported in that one season, being allured by the stench, and daily fed by the dead carcasses thrown overboard on the voyage."

If the reader should observe here, that cattle are better protected in this country, than slaves in the colonies, his observation will be just. The beast which is driven to market, is defended by law from the goad of the driver; whereas the wretched African, though an human being, and whose feelings receive of course a double poignancy from the power of reflection, is unnoticed in this respect in the colonial code, and may be goaded and beaten till he expires.

We may now take our leave of the *first receivers*. Their crime has been already estimated; and to reason farther upon it, would be unnecessary. For where the conduct of men is so manifestly impious, there can be no need, either of a single argument or a reflection; as every reader of sensibility will anticipate them in his own feelings.

Chapter 3

When the wretched Africans are thus put into the hands of the second *receivers*, they are conveyed to the plantations, where they are totally considered as *cattle*, or *beasts of labour*; their very children, if any should be born to them in that situation, being previously destined to the condition of their parents. But here a question arises, which, will interrupt the thread of the narration for a little time, viz. how far their descendants, who compose the fifth order of slaves, are justly reduced to servitude, and upon what principles the *receivers* defend their conduct.

Authors have been at great pains to inquire, why, in the ancient servitude, the child has uniformly followed the condition of the mother. But we conceive that they would have saved themselves much trouble, and have done themselves more credit, if instead of, endeavouring to reconcile the custom with *heathen* notions, or their own laboured conjectures, they had shewn its inconsistency with reason and nature, and its repugnancy to common justice. Suffice it to say, that the whole theory of the ancients, with respect to the descendants slaves, may be reduced to this principle, "that as the parents, by becoming *property*, were wholly considered as *cattle*, their children, like *the progeny of cattle*, inherited their parental lot."

Such also is the excuse of the tyrannical *receivers* beforementioned. They allege, that they have purchased the parents, that they can sell and dispose of them as they please, that they possess them under the same laws and limitations as their cattle, and that their children, like the progeny of these, become their property *by birth*.

But the absurdity of the argument will immediately appear. It depends wholly on the supposition, that the parents are *brutes*. If they are *brutes*, we shall instantly cease to contend: if they are *men*, which we think it not difficult to prove, the argument must immediately fall, as we have already shewn that there cannot justly be any *property* whatever in the *human species*.

It has appeared also, in the second part of this Essay, that as nature made, every man's body and mind *his own*, so no *just* person can be reduced to slavery against his own *consent*. Do the unfortunate offspring ever *consent* to be slaves?-They are slaves from their birth.-Are they *guilty* of crimes, that they lose their freedom?-They are slaves when they cannot speak.-Are their *parents* abandoned? The crimes of the parents cannot justly extend to the children.

Thus then must the tyrannical *receivers*, who presume to sentence the children of slaves to servitude, if they mean to dispute upon the justice of their cause; either allow them to have been *brutes* from their birth, or to have been guilty of crimes at a time, when they were incapable of offending the very *King of Kings*.

Chapter 4

But to return to the narration. When the wretched Africans are conveyed to the plantations, they are considered as *beasts of labour*, and are put to their respective work. Having led, in their own country, a life of indolence and ease, where the earth brings forth spontaneously the comforts of life, and spares frequently the toil and trouble of cultivation, they can hardly be expected to endure the drudgeries of servitude. Calculations are accordingly made upon their lives. It is conjectured, that if three in four survive what is called the *seasoning*, the bargain is highly favourable. This seasoning is said to expire, when the two first years of their servitude are completed: It is the time which an African must take to be so accustomed to the colony, as to be able to endure the common labour of a plantation, and to be put into the *gang*. At the end of this period the calculations become verified, twenty thousand[59] of those, who are annually imported, dying before the seasoning is over. This is surely an horrid and awful consideration: and thus does it appear, (and let it be remembered, that it is the lowest calculation that has been ever made upon the subject) that out of every annual supply that is shipped from the coast of Africa, *forty thousand lives*[60] are regularly expended, even before it can be said, that there is really any additional stock for the colonies.

When the seasoning is over, and the survivors are thus enabled to endure the usual task of slaves, they are considered as real and substantial supplies. From this period[61] therefore we shall describe their situation.

They are summoned at five in the morning to begin their work. This work may be divided into two kinds, the culture of the fields, and the collection of grass for cattle. The last is the most laborious and intolerable employment; as the grass can only be collected blade by blade, and is to be fetched frequently twice a day at a considerable distance from the plantation. In these two occupations they are jointly taken up, with no other intermission than that of taking their subsistence twice, till nine at night. They then separate for their respective huts, when they gather sticks, prepare their supper, and attend their families. This employs them till midnight, when they go to rest. Such is their daily way of life for rather more than half the year. They are *sixteen* hours, including two intervals at meals, in the service of their masters: they are employed *three* afterwards in their own necessary concerns; *five* only remain for sleep, and their day is finished.

During the remaining portion of the year, or the time of crop, the nature, as well as the time of their employment, is considerably changed. The whole gang is generally divided into two or three bodies. One of these, besides the ordinary labour of the day, is kept in turn at the mills, that are constantly going, during the whole of the night. This is a dreadful encroachment upon their time of rest, which was before too short to permit them perfectly to refresh their wearied limbs, and actually reduces their sleep, as long as this season lasts, to about three hours and an half a night, upon a moderate computation.[62] Those who can keep their eyes open during their nightly labour, and are willing to resist the drowsiness that is continually coming upon them, are presently worn out; while some of those, who are overcome, and who feed the mill between asleep and awake, suffer, for thus obeying the calls of nature, by the loss of a limb.[63] In this manner they go on, with little or no respite from their work, till the crop season is over, when the year (from the time of our first description) is completed.

To support[64] a life of such unparalleled drudgery, we should at least expect: to find, that they were comfortably clothed, and plentifully fed. But sad reverse! they have scarcely a covering to defend themselves against the inclemency of the night. Their provisions are frequently bad, and are always dealt out to them with such a sparing hand, that the means of a bare livelihood are not placed within the reach of four out of five of these unhappy people. It is a fact, that many of the disorders of slaves are contracted from eating the vegetables, which their little spots produce, before they are sufficiently ripe: a clear indication, that the calls of hunger are frequently so pressing, as not to suffer them to wait, till they can really enjoy them.

This, situation, of a want of the common necessaries of life, added to that of hard and continual labour, must be sufficiently painful of itself. How then must the pain be sharpened, if it be accompanied with severity! if an unfortunate slave does not come into the field exactly at the appointed time, if, drooping with sickness or fatigue, he appears to work unwillingly, or if the bundle of grass that he has been collecting, appears too small in the eye of the overseer, he is equally sure of experiencing the whip. This instrument erases the skin, and cuts out small portions of the flesh at almost every stroke; and is so frequently applied, that the smack of it is all day long in the ears of those, who are in the vicinity of the plantations. This severity of masters, or managers, to their slaves, which is considered only as common discipline, is attended with bad effects. It enables them to behold instances of cruelty without commiseration, and to be guilty of them without remorse. Hence those many acts of deliberate mutilation, that have taken place on the slightest occasions: hence those many acts of inferiour, though shocking, barbarity, that have taken place without any occasion at all: the very slitting[65] of ears has been considered as an operation, so perfectly devoid of pain, as to have been performed for no other reason than that for which a brand is set upon cattle, *as a mark of property.*

But this is not the only effect, which this severity produces: for while it hardens their hearts, and makes them insensible of the misery of their fellow-creatures, it begets a turn for wanton cruelty. As a proof of this, we shall mention one, among the many instances that occur, where ingenuity has been exerted in contriving modes of torture. "An iron coffin, with holes in it, was kept by a certain colonist, as an auxiliary to the lash. In this the poor victim of the master's resentment was inclosed, and placed sufficiently near a fire, to occasion extreme pain, and consequently shrieks and groans, until the revenge of the master was satiated, without any other inconvenience on his part, than a temporary suspension of the slave's labour. Had he been flogged to death, or his limbs mutilated, the interest of the brutal tyrant would have suffered a more irreparable loss.

"In mentioning, this instance, we do not mean to insinuate, that it is common. We know that it was reprobated by many. All that we would infer from it is, that where men are habituated to a system of severity, they become *wantonly cruel,* and that the mere toleration of such an instrument of torture, in any country, is a clear indication, *that this wretched class of men do not there enjoy the protection of any laws, that may be pretended to have been enacted in their favour.*"

Such then is the general situation of the unfortunate Africans. They are beaten and tortured at discretion. They are badly clothed. They are miserably fed. Their drudgery is intense and incessant and their rest short. For scarcely are their heads reclined, scarcely have their bodies a respite from the labour of the day, or the cruel hand of the overseer, but they are summoned to renew their sorrows. In this manner they go on from year to year, in a state of the lowest degradation, without a single law to protect them, without the possibility of redress, without a hope that their situation will be changed, unless death should terminate the scene.

Having described the general situation of these unfortunate people, we shall now take notice of the common consequences that are found to attend it, and relate them separately, as they result either from long and painful *labour*, a *want* of the common necessaries of life, or continual *severity*.

Oppressed by a daily task of such immoderate labour as human nature is utterly unable to perform, many of them run away from their masters. They fly to the recesses of the mountains, where they choose rather to live upon any thing that the soil affords them, nay, the very soil itself, than return to that *happy situation*, which is represented by the *receivers*, as the condition of a slave.

It sometimes happens, that the manager of a mountain plantation, falls in with one of these; he immediately seizes him, and threatens to carry him to his former master, unless he will consent to live on the mountain and cultivate his ground. When his plantation is put in order, he carries the delinquent home, abandons him to all the suggestions of despotick rage, and accepts a reward for his *honesty*. The unhappy wretch is chained, scourged, tortured; and all this, because he obeyed the dictates of nature, and wanted to be free. And who is there, that would not have done the same thing, in the same situation? Who is there, that has once known the charms of liberty; that would not fly from despotism? And yet, by the impious laws of the *receivers*, the absence[66] of six months from the lash of tyranny is-*death*.

But this law is even mild, when compared with another against the same offence, which was in force sometime ago, and which we fear is even now in force, in some of those colonies which this account of the treatment comprehends. "Advertisements have frequently appeared there, offering a reward for the apprehending of fugitive slaves either alive or *dead*. The following instance was given us by a person of unquestionable veracity, under whose own observation it fell. As he was travelling in one of the colonies alluded to, he observed some people in pursuit of a poor wretch, who was seeking in the wilderness an asylum from his labours. He heard the discharge of a gun, and soon afterwards stopping at an house for refreshment, the head of the fugitive, still reeking with blood, was brought in and laid upon a table with exultation. The production of such a trophy was the proof *required by law* to entitle the heroes to their reward." Now reader determine if you can, who were the most execrable; the rulers of the state in authorizing murder, or the people in being bribed to commit it.

This is one of the common consequences of that immoderate share of labour, which is imposed upon them; nor is that, which is the result of a scanty allowance of food, less to be lamented. The wretched African is often so deeply pierced by the excruciating fangs of hunger, as almost to be driven to despair. What is he to do in such a trying situation? Let him apply to the *receivers*. Alas! the majesty of *receivership* is too sacred for the appeal, and the intrusion would be fatal. Thus attacked on the one hand, and shut out from every possibility of relief on the other, he has only the choice of being starved, or of relieving his necessities by taking a small portion of the fruits of his own labour. Horrid crime! to be found eating the cane, which probably his own hands have planted, and to be eating it, because his necessities were pressing! This crime however is of such a magnitude, as always to be accompanied with the whip; and so unmercifully has it been applied on such an occasion, as to have been the cause, in wet weather, of the delinquent's death. But the smart of the whip has not been the only pain that the wretched Africans have experienced. Any thing that passion could seize, and convert into an instrument of punishment, has been used; and, horrid to relate! the very knife has not been overlooked in the fit of phrenzy. Ears have been slit, eyes have been beaten out, and bones have been broken; and so frequently has this been the case, that it has been a matter of constant lamentation with disinterested people, who out of curiosity have attended the markets[67] to which these unhappy people weekly resort, that they have not been able to turn their eyes on any group of them whatever, but they have beheld these inhuman marks of passion, despotism, and caprice.

But these instances of barbarity have not been able to deter them from similar proceedings. And indeed, how can it be expected that they should? They have still the same appetite to be satisfied as before, and to drive them to desperation. They creep out clandestinely by night, and go in search of food into their master's, or some neighbouring plantation. But here they are almost equally sure of suffering. The watchman, who will be punished himself, if he neglects his duty, frequently seizes them in the fact. No excuse or intreaty will avail; he must punish them for an example, and he must punish them, not with a stick, nor with a whip, but with a cutlass. Thus it happens, that these unhappy slaves, if they are taken, are either sent away mangled in a barbarous manner, or are killed upon the spot.

We may now mention the consequences of the severity. The wretched Africans, daily subjected to the lash, and unmercifully whipt and beaten on every trifling occasion, have been found to resist their opposers. Unpardonable crime! that they should have the feelings of nature! that their breasts should glow with resentment on an injury! that they should be so far overcome, as to resist those, whom *they are under no obligations to obey*, and whose only title to their services consists in *a violation of the rights of men*! What has been the consequence?-But here let us spare the feelings of the reader, (we wish we could spare our own) and let us only say, without a recital of the cruelty, *that they have been murdered at the discretion of their masters.* For let the reader observe, that the life of an African is only valued at a price, that would scarcely purchase an horse; that the master has a power of murdering his slave, if he pays but a trifling fine; and that the murder must be attended with uncommon circumstances of horrour, if it even produces an inquiry.

Immortal Alfred! father of our invaluable constitution! parent of the civil blessings we enjoy! how ought thy laws to excite our love and veneration, who hast forbidden us, thy posterity, to tremble at the frown of tyrants! how ought they to perpetuate thy name, as venerable, to the remotest ages, who has secured, even to the meanest servant, a fair and impartial trial! How much does nature approve thy laws, as consistent with her own feelings, while she absolutely turns pale, trembles, and recoils, at the institutions of these *receivers*! Execrable men! you do not murder the horse, on which you only ride; you do not mutilate the cow, which only affords you her milk; you do not torture the dog, which is but a partial servant of your pleasures: but these unfortunate men, from whom, you derive your very pleasures and your fortunes, you torture, mutilate, murder at discretion! Sleep then you *receivers*, if you can, while you scarcely allow these unfortunate people to rest at all! feast if you can, and indulge your genius, while you daily apply to these unfortunate people the stings of severity and hunger! exult in riches, at which even avarice ought to shudder, and, which humanity must detest!

Chapter 5

Some people may suppose, from the melancholy account that has been given in the preceding chapter, that we have been absolutely dealing in romance: that the scene exhibited is rather a dreary picture of the imagination, than a representation of fact. Would to heaven, for the honour of human nature, that this were really the case! We wish we could say, that we have no testimony to produce for any of our assertions, and that our description of the general treatment of slaves has been greatly exaggerated.

But the *receivers*, notwithstanding the ample and disinterested evidence, that can be brought on the occasion, do not admit the description to be true. They say first, "that if the slavery were such as has been now represented, no human being could possibly support it long." Melancholy truth! the wretched Africans generally perish in their prime. Let them reflect upon the prodigious supplies that are *annually* required, and their argument will be nothing less than a confession, that the slavery has been justly depicted.

They appeal next to every man's own reason, and desire him to think seriously, whether "self-interest will not always restrain the master from acts of cruelty to the slave, and whether such accounts therefore, as the foregoing, do not contain within themselves, their own refutation." We answer, "No." For if this restraining principle be as powerful as it is imagined, why does not the general conduct of men afford us a better picture? What is imprudence, or what is vice, but a departure from every man's own interest, and yet these are the characteristicks of more than half the world?-

-But, to come more closely to the present case, *self-interest* will be found but a weak barrier against the sallies of *passion*: particularly where it has been daily indulged in its greatest latitude, and there are no laws to restrain its calamitous effects. If the observation be true, that passion is a short madness, then it is evident that self-interest, and every other consideration, must be lost, so long as it continues. We cannot have a stronger instance of this, than in a circumstance related in the second part of this Essay, "that though the Africans have gone to war for the express purpose of procuring slaves, yet so great has been their resentment at the resistance they have frequently found, that their *passion* has entirely got the better of their *interest*, and they have murdered all without any discrimination, either of age or sex." Such may be presumed to be the case with the no less savage *receivers*. Impressed with the most haughty and tyrannical notions, easily provoked, accustomed to indulge their anger, and, above all, habituated to scenes of cruelty, and unawed by the fear of laws, they will hardly be found to be exempt from the common failings of human nature, and to spare an unlucky slave, at a time when men of cooler temper, and better regulated passions, are so frequently blind to their own interest.

But if *passion* may be supposed to be generally more than a ballance for *interest*, how must the scale be turned in favour of the melancholy picture exhibited, when we reflect that *self-preservation* additionally steps in, and demands the most *rigorous severity*. For when we consider that where there is *one* master, there are *fifty* slaves; that the latter have been all forcibly torn from their country, and are retained in their present situation by violence; that they are perpetually at war in their hearts with their oppressors, and are continually cherishing the seeds of revenge; it is evident that even *avarice* herself, however cool and deliberate, however free from passion and caprice, must sacrifice her own sordid feelings, and adopt a system of tyranny and oppression, which it must be ruinous to pursue.

Thus then, if no picture had been drawn of the situation of slaves, and it had been left solely to every man's sober judgment to determine, what it might probably be, he would conclude, that if the situation were justly described, the page must be frequently stained with acts of uncommon cruelty.

It remains only to make a reply to an objection, that is usually advanced against particular instances of cruelty to slaves, as recorded by various writers. It is said that "some of these are so inconceivably, and beyond all example inhuman, that their very excess above the common measure of cruelty shews them at once exaggerated and incredible." But their credibility shall be estimated by a supposition. Let us suppose that the following instance had been recorded by a writer of the highest reputation, "that the master of a ship, bound to the western colonies with slaves, on a presumption that many of them would die, selected an *hundred and thirty two* of the most sickly, and ordered them to be thrown into the sea, to recover their value from the insurers, and, above all, that the fatal order was put into execution." What would the reader have thought on the occasion? Would he have believed the fact? It would have surely staggered his faith; because he could never have heard that any *one* man ever was, and could never have supposed that any *one* man ever could be, guilty of the murder of *such a number* of his fellow creatures. But when he is informed that such a fact as this came before a court[68] of justice in this very country; that it happened within the last five years; that hundreds can come forwards and say, that they heard the melancholy evidence with tears; what bounds is he to place to his belief? The great God, who looks down upon all his creatures with the same impartial eye, seems to have infatuated the parties concerned, that they might bring the horrid circumstance to light, that it might be recorded in the annals of a publick court, as an authentick specimen of the treatment which the unfortunate Africans undergo, and at the same time, as an argument to shew, that there is no species of cruelty, that is recorded to have been exercised upon these wretched people, so enormous that it may not *readily be believed*.

Chapter 6

If the treatment then, as before described, is confirmed by reason, and the great credit that is due to disinterested writers on the subject; if the unfortunate Africans are used, as if their flesh were stone, and their vitals brass; by what arguments do you *receivers* defend your conduct?

You say that a great part of your savage treatment consists in punishment for real offences, and frequently for such offences, as all civilized nations have concurred in punishing. The first charge that you exhibit against them is specifick, it is that of *theft*. But how much rather ought you *receivers* to blush, who reduce them to such a situation! who reduce them to the dreadful alternative, that they must either *steal* or *perish*! How much rather ought you *receivers* to be considered as *robbers* yourselves, who cause these unfortunate people to be *stolen*! And how much greater is your crime, who are *robbers of human liberty*!

The next charge which you exhibit against them, is general, it is that of *rebellion*; a crime of such a latitude, that you can impose it upon almost every action, and of such a nature, that you always annex to it the most excruciating pain. But what a contradiction is this to common sense! Have the wretched Africans formally resigned their freedom? Have you any other claim upon their obedience, than that of force? If then they are your subjects, you violate the laws of government, by making them unhappy. But if they are not your subjects, then, even though they should resist your proceedings, they are not *rebellious*.

But what do you say to that long catalogue of offences, which you punish, and of which no people but yourselves take cognizance at all? You say that the wisdom of legislation has inserted it in the colonial laws, and that you punish by authority. But do you allude to that execrable code, that *authorises murder*? that tempts an unoffended person to kill the slave, that abhors and flies your service? that delegates a power, which no host of men, which not all the world, can possess?-

Or,-What do you say to that daily unmerited severity, which you consider only as common discipline? Here you say that the Africans are vicious, that they are all of them ill-disposed, that you must of necessity be severe. But can they be well-disposed to their oppressors? In their own country they were just, generous, hospitable: qualities, which all the African historians allow them eminently to possess. If then they are vicious, they must have contracted many of their vices from yourselves; and as to their own native vices, if any have been imported with them, are they not amiable, when compared with yours?

Thus then do the excuses, which have been hitherto made by the *receivers*, force a relation of such circumstances, as makes their conduct totally inexcusable, and, instead of diminishing at all, highly aggravates their guilt.

Chapter 7

We come now to that other system of reasoning, which is always applied, when the former is confuted; "that the Africans are an inferiour link of the chain of nature, and are made for slavery."

This assertion is proved by two arguments; the first of which was advanced also by the ancients, and is drawn from the *inferiority of their capacities*.

Let us allow then for a moment, that they appear to have no parts, that they appear to be void of understanding. And is this wonderful, when, you *receivers* depress their senses by hunger? Is this wonderful, when by incessant labour, the continual application of the lash, and the most inhuman treatment that imagination can devise, you overwhelm their genius, and hinder it from breaking forth?-No,-You confound their abilities by the severity of their servitude: for as a spark of fire, if crushed by too great a weight of incumbent fuel, cannot be blown into a flame, but suddenly expires, so the human mind, if depressed by rigorous servitude, cannot be excited to a display of those faculties, which might otherwise have shone with the brightest lustre.

Neither is it wonderful in another point of view. For what is it that awakens the abilities of men, and distinguishes them from the common herd? Is it not often the amiable hope of becoming serviceable to individuals, or the state? Is it not often the hope of riches, or of power? Is it not frequently the hope of temporary honours, or a lasting fame? These principles have all a wonderful effect upon the mind. They call upon it to exert its faculties, and bring those talents to the publick view, which had otherwise been concealed. But the unfortunate Africans have no such incitements as these, that they should shew their genius. They have no hope of riches, power, honours, fame. They have no hope but this, that their miseries will be soon terminated by death.

And here we cannot but censure and expose the murmurings of the unthinking and the gay; who, going on in a continual round of pleasure and prosperity, repine at the will of Providence, as exhibited in the shortness of human duration. But let a weak and infirm old age overtake them: let them experience calamities: let them feel but half the miseries which the wretched Africans undergo, and they will praise the goodness of Providence, who hath made them mortal; who hath prescribed certain ordinary bounds to the life of man; and who, by such a limitation, hath given all men this comfortable hope, that however persecuted in life, a time will come, in the common course of nature, when their sufferings will have an end.

Such then is the nature of this servitude, that we can hardly expect to find in those, who undergo it, even the glimpse of genius. For if their minds are in a continual state of depression, and if they have no expectations in life to awaken their abilities, and make them eminent, we cannot be surprized if a sullen gloomy stupidity should be the leading mark in their character; or if they should appear inferiour to those, who do not only enjoy the invaluable blessings of freedom, but have every prospect before their eyes, that can allure them to exert their faculties. Now, if to these considerations we add, that the wretched Africans are torn from their country in a state of nature, and that in general, as long as their slavery continues, every obstacle is placed in the way of their improvement, we shall have a sufficient answer to any argument that may be drawn from the inferiority of their capacities.

It appears then, from the circumstances that have been mentioned, that to form a true judgment of the abilities of these unfortunate people, we must either take a general view of them before their slavery commences, or confine our attention to such, as, after it has commenced, have had any opportunity given them of shewing their genius either in arts or letters. If, upon such a fair and impartial view, there should be any reason to suppose, that they are at all inferiour to others in the same situation, the argument will then gain some of that weight and importance, which it wants at present.

In their own country, where we are to see them first, we must expect that the prospect will be unfavourable. They are mostly in a savage state. Their powers of mind are limited to few objects. Their ideas are consequently few. It appears, however, that they follow the same mode of life, and exercise the same arts, as the ancestors of those very Europeans, who boast of their great superiority, are described to have done in the same uncultivated state. This appears from the Nubian's Geography, the writings of Leo, the Moor, and all the subsequent histories, which those, who have visited the African continent, have written from their own inspection. Hence three conclusions;

that their abilities are sufficient for their situation;-that they are as great, as those of other people have been, in the same stage of society;-and that they are as great as those of any civilized people whatever, when the degree of the barbarism of the one is drawn into a comparison with that of the civilization of the other.

Let us now follow them to the colonies. They are carried over in the unfavourable situation described. It is observed here, that though their abilities cannot be estimated high from a want of cultivation, they are yet various, and that they vary in proportion as the nation, from which they have been brought, has advanced more or less in the scale of social life. This observation, which is so frequently made, is of great importance: for if their abilities expand in proportion to the improvement of their state, it is a clear indication, that if they were equally improved, they would be equally ingenious.

But here, before we consider any opportunities that may be afforded them, let it be remembered that even their most polished situation may be called barbarous, and that this circumstance, should they appear less docile than others, may be considered as a sufficient answer to any objection that may be made to their capacities. Notwithstanding this, when they are put to the mechanical arts, they do not discover a want of ingenuity. They attain them in as short a time as the Europeans, and arrive at a degree of excellence equal to that of their teachers. This is a fact, almost universally known, and affords us this proof, that having learned with facility such of the mechanical arts, as they have been taught, they are capable of attaining any other, at least, of the same class, if they should receive but the same instruction.

With respect to the liberal arts, their proficiency is certainly less; but not less in proportion to their time and opportunity of study; not less, because they are less capable of attaining them, but because they have seldom or ever an opportunity of learning them at all. It is yet extraordinary that their talents appear, even in some of these sciences, in which they are totally uninstructed. Their abilities in musick are such, as to have been generally noticed. They play frequently upon a variety of instruments, without any other assistance than their own ingenuity. They have also tunes of their own composition. Some of these have been imported among us; are now in use; and are admired for their sprightliness and ease, though the ungenerous and prejudiced importer has concealed their original.

Neither are their talents in poetry less conspicuous. Every occurrence, if their spirits are not too greatly depressed, is turned into a song. These songs are said to be incoherent and nonsensical. But this proceeds principally from two causes, an improper conjunction of words, arising from an ignorance of the language in which they compose; and a wildness of thought, arising from the different manner, in which the organs of rude and civilized people will be struck by the same object. And as to their want of harmony and rhyme, which is the last objection, the difference of pronunciation is the cause. Upon the whole, as they are perfectly consistent with their own ideas, and are strictly musical as pronounced by themselves, they afford us as high a proof of their poetical powers, as the works of the most acknowledged poets.

But where these impediments have been removed, where they have received an education, and have known and pronounced the language with propriety, these defects have vanished, and their productions have been less objectionable. For a proof of this, we appeal to the writings of an African girl,[69] who made no contemptible appearance in this species of composition. She was kidnapped when only eight years old, and, in the year 1761, was transported to America, where she was sold with other slaves. She had no school education there, but receiving some little instruction from the family, with whom she was so fortunate as to live, she obtained such a knowledge of the English language within sixteen months from the time of her arrival, as to be able to speak it and read it to the astonishment of those who heard her. She soon afterwards learned to write, and, having a great inclination to learn the Latin tongue, she was indulged by her master, and made a progress. Her Poetical works were published with his permission, in the year 1773. They contain thirty-eight pieces on different subjects. We shall beg leave to make a short extract from two or three of them, for the observation of the reader.

From an Hymn to the Evening.[70]

"Fill'd with the praise of him who gives the light,
And draws the sable curtains of the night,
Let placid slumbers sooth each weary mind,
At morn to wake more heav'nly and refin'd;
So shall the labours of the day begin,
More pure and guarded from the snares of sin.
- - &c. &c."

From an Hymn to the Morning.

CLARKSON

"Aurora hail! and all the thousand dies,
That deck thy progress through the vaulted skies!
The morn awakes, and wide extends her rays,
On ev'ry leaf the gentle zephyr plays.
Harmonious lays the feather'd race resume,
Dart the bright eye, and shake the painted plume.
- - &c. &c."

From Thoughts on Imagination.

"Now here, now there, the roving *fancy* flies,
Till some lov'd object strikes her wand'ring eyes,
Whose silken fetters all the senses bind,
And soft captivity involves the mind.

"*Imagination!* who can sing thy force,
Or who describe the swiftness of thy course?
Soaring through air to find the bright abode,
Th' empyreal palace of the thund'ring God,
We on thy pinions can surpass the wind,
And leave the rolling universe behind:
From star to star the mental opticks rove,
Measure the skies, and range the realms above.
There in one view we grasp the mighty whole,
Or with new worlds amaze th' unbounded soul.
- - &c. &c."

Such is the poetry which we produce as a proof of our assertions.
How far it has succeeded, the reader may by this time have determined
in his own mind. We shall therefore only beg leave to accompany it
with this observation, that if the authoress *was designed for slavery*,
(as the argument must confess) the greater part of the inhabitants of
Britain must lose their claim to freedom.

To this poetry we shall only add, as a farther proof of their abilities, the Prose compositions of Ignatius Sancho, who received some
little education. His letters are too well known, to make any extract, or
indeed any farther mention of him, necessary. If other examples of
African genius should be required, suffice it to say, that they can be
produced in abundance; and that if we were allowed to enumerate instances of African gratitude, patience, fidelity, honour, as so many

instances of good sense, and a sound understanding, we fear that thousands of the enlightened Europeans would have occasion to blush.

But an objection will be made here, that the two persons whom we have particularized by name, are prodigies, and that if we were to live for many years, we should scarcely meet with two other Africans of the same description. But we reply, that considering their situation as before described, two persons, above mediocrity in the literary way, are as many as can be expected within a certain period of years; and farther, that if these are prodigies, they are only such prodigies as every day would produce, if they had the same opportunities of acquiring knowledge as other people, and the same expectations in life to excite their genius. This has been constantly and solemnly asserted by the pious Benezet,[71] whom we have mentioned before, as having devoted a considerable part of his time to their instruction. This great man, for we cannot but mention him with veneration, had a better opportunity of knowing them than any person whatever, and he always uniformly declared, that he could never find a difference between their capacities and those of other people; that they were as capable of reasoning as any individual Europeans; that they were as capable of the highest intellectual attainments; in short, that their abilities were equal, and that they only wanted to be equally cultivated, to afford specimens of as fine productions.

Thus then does it appear from the testimony of this venerable man, whose authority is sufficient of itself to silence all objections against African capacity, and from the instances that have been produced, and the observations that have been made on the occasion, that if the minds of the Africans were unbroken by slavery; if they had the same expectations in life as other people, and the same opportunities of improvement, they would be equal; in all the various branches of science, to the Europeans, and that the argument that states them "to be an inferiour link of the chain of nature, and designed for servitude," as far as it depends on the *inferiority of their capacities*, is wholly malevolent and false.[72]

Chapter 8

The second argument, by which it is attempted to be proved, "that the Africans are an inferiour link of the chain of nature, and are designed for slavery," is drawn from *colour*, and from those other marks, which distinguish them from the inhabitants of Europe.

To prove this with the greater facility, the *receivers* divide in opinion. Some of them contend that the Africans, from these circumstances, are the descendants of Cain:[73] others, that they are the posterity of Ham; and that as it was declared by divine inspiration, that these should be servants to the rest of the world, so they are designed for slavery; and that the reducing of them to such a situation is only the accomplishment of the will of heaven: while the rest, considering them from the same circumstances as a totally distinct species of men, conclude them to be an inferiour link of the chain of nature, and deduce the inference described.

To answer these arguments in the clearest and fullest manner, we are under the necessity of making two suppositions, first, that the scriptures are true; secondly, that they are false.

If then the scriptures are true, it is evident that the posterity of Cain were extinguished in the flood. Thus one of the arguments is no more.

With respect to the curse of Ham, it appears also that it was limited; that it did not extend to the posterity of all his sons, but only to the descendants of him who was called Canaan:[74] by which it was foretold that the Canaanites, a part of the posterity of Ham, should serve the posterity of Shem and Japhet. Now how does it appear that these wretched Africans are the descendants of Canaan?-By those marks, it will be said, which distinguish them from the rest of the world.-But where are these marks to be found in the divine writings? In what page is it said, that the Canaanites were to be known by their *colour*, their *features*, their *form*, or the very *hair of their heads*, which is brought into the account?-But alas! so far are the divine writings from giving any such account, that they shew the assertion to be false. They shew that the descendants of Cush[75] were of the colour, to which the advocates for slavery allude; and of course, that there was no such limitation of colour to the posterity of Canaan, or the inheritors of the curse.

Suppose we should now shew, upon the most undeniable evidence,[76] that those of the wretched Africans, who are singled out as inheriting the curse, are the descendants of Cush or Phut; and that we should shew farther, that but a single remnant of Canaan, which was afterwards ruined, was ever in Africa at all.-Here all is consternation.-

But unfortunately again for the argument, though wonderfully for the confirmation that the scriptures are of divine original, the whole prophecy has been completed. A part of the descendants of Canaan were hewers of wood and drawers of water, and became tributary and subject to the Israelites, or the descendants of Shem. The Greeks afterwards, as well as the Romans, who were both the descendants of Japhet, not only subdued those who were settled in Syria and Palestine, but pursued and conquered all such as were then remaining. These were the Tyrians and Carthaginians: the former of whom were ruined by Alexander and the Greeks, the latter by Scipio and the Romans.

It appears then that the second argument is wholly inapplicable and false: that it is false in its *application*, because those, who were the objects of the curse, were a totally distinct people: that it is false in its *proof*, because no such distinguishing marks, as have been specified, are to be found in the divine writings: and that, if the proof could be made out, it would be now *inapplicable*, as the curse has been long completed.

With respect to the third argument, we must now suppose that the scriptures are false; that mankind did not all spring from the same original; that there are different species of men. Now what must we justly conclude from such a supposition? Must we conclude that one species is inferiour to another, and that the inferiority depends upon their *colour*, or their *features*, or their *form*?-No-We must now consult the analogy of nature, and the conclusion will be this: "that as she tempered the bodies of the different species of men in a different degree, to enable them to endure the respective climates of their habitation, so she gave them a variety of colour and appearance with a like benevolent design."

To sum up the whole. If the scriptures are true, it is evident that the posterity of *Cain* are no more; that the curse of *Ham* has been accomplished; and that, as all men were derived from the same stock, so this variety of appearance in men must either have proceeded from some interposition of the Deity; or from a co-operation of certain causes, which have an effect upon the human frame, and have the power of changing it more or less from its primitive appearance, as they happen to be more or less numerous or powerful than those, which acted upon the frame of man in the first seat of his habitation. If from the interposition of the Deity, then we must conclude that he, who bringeth good out of evil, produced it for their convenience. If, from the co-operation of the causes before related, what argument may not be found against any society of men, who should happen to differ, in the points alluded to, from ourselves?

If, on the other hand, the scriptures are false, then it is evident, that there was neither such a person as *Cain*, nor *Ham*, nor *Canaan*; and that nature bestowed such colour, features, and form, upon the different species of men, as were best adapted to their situation.

Thus, on which ever supposition it is founded, the whole argument must fall. And indeed it is impossible that it can stand, even in the eye of common sense. For if you admit the *form* of men as a justification of slavery, you may subjugate your own brother: if *features*, then you must quarrel with all the world: if *colour*, where are you to stop? It is evident, that if you travel from the equator to the northern pole, you will find a regular gradation of colour from black to white. Now if you can justly take him for your slave, who is of the deepest die, what hinders you from taking him also, who only differs from the former but by a shade. Thus you may proceed, taking each in a regular succession to the poles. But who are you, that thus take into slavery so many people? Where do you live yourself? Do you live in *Spain*, or in *France*, or in *Britain*? If in either of these countries, take care lest the *whiter natives of the north* should have a claim upon yourself.-But the argument is too ridiculous to be farther noticed.

Having now silenced the whole argument, we might immediately proceed to the discussion of other points, without even declaring our opinion as to which of the suppositions may be right, on which it has been refuted; but we do not think ourselves at liberty to do this. The present age would rejoice to find that the scriptures had no foundation, and would anxiously catch at the writings of him, who should mention them in a doubtful manner. We shall therefore declare our sentiments, by asserting that they are true, and that all mankind, however various their appearances are derived from the same stock.

To prove this, we shall not produce those innumerable arguments, by which the scriptures have stood the test of ages, but advert to a single fact. It is an universal law, observable throughout the whole creation, *that if two animals of a different species propagate, their offspring is unable to continue its own species.* By this admirable law, the different species are preserved distinct; every possibility of confusion is prevented, and the world is forbidden to be over-run by a race of monsters. Now, if we apply this law to those of the human kind, who are said to be of a distinct species from each other, it immediately fails. The *mulattoe* is as capable of continuing his own species as his father; a clear and irrefragable proof, that the scripture[77] account of the creation is true, and that "God, who hath made the world, hath made of one blood[78] all the nations of men that dwell on all the face of the earth."

But if this be the case, it will be said that mankind were originally of one colour; and it will be asked at the same time, what it is probable that the colour was, and how they came to assume so various an appearance? To, each of these we shall make that reply, which we conceive to be the most rational.

As mankind were originally of the same stock, so it is evident that they were originally of the same colour. But how shall we attempt to ascertain it? Shall we *Englishmen* say, that it was the same as that which we now find to be peculiar to ourselves?-No-This would be a vain and partial consideration, and would betray our judgment to have arisen from that false fondness, which habituates us to suppose, that every thing belonging to ourselves is the perfectest and the best. Add to this, that we should always be liable to a just reproof from every inhabitant of the globe, whose colour was different from our own; because he would justly say, that he had as good a right to imagine that his own was the primitive colour, as that of any other people.

How then shall we attempt to ascertain it? Shall we look into the various climates of the earth, see the colour that generally prevails in the inhabitants of each, and apply the rule? This will be certainly free from partiality, and will afford us a better prospect of success: for as every particular district has its particular colour, so it is evident that the complexion of Noah and his sons, from whom the rest of the world were descended, was the same as that, which is peculiar to the country, which was the seat of their habitation. This, by such a mode of decision, will be found a dark olive; a beautiful colour, and a just medium between white and black. That this was the primitive colour, is highly probable from the observations that have been made; and, if admitted, will afford a valuable lesson to the Europeans, to be cautious how they deride those of the opposite complexion, as there is great reason to presume, *that the purest white*[79] *is as far removed from the primitive colour as the deepest black.*

We come now to the grand question, which is, that if mankind were originally of this or any other colour, how came it to pass, that they should wear so various an appearance? We reply, as we have had occasion to say before, either *by the interposition of the Deity*; or *by a co-operation of certain causes, which have an effect upon the human frame, and have the power of changing it more or less from its primitive appearance, as they are more or less numerous or powerful than those, which acted upon the frame of man in the first seat of his habitation.*

With respect to the Divine interposition, two epochs have been assigned, when this difference of colour has been imagined to have been so produced. The first is that, which has been related, when the curse was pronounced on a branch of the posterity of *Ham*. But this argument has been already refuted; for if the particular colour alluded to were assigned at this period, it was assigned to the descendants of *Canaan*, to distinguish them from those of his other brothers, and was therefore *limited* to the former. But the descendants of *Cush*,[80] as we have shewn before, partook of the same colour; a clear proof, that it was neither assigned to them on this occasion, nor at this period.

The second epoch is that, when mankind were dispersed on the building of *Babel*. It has been thought, that both *national features and colour* might probably have been given them at this time, because these would have assisted the confusion of language, by causing them to disperse into tribes, and would have united more firmly the individuals of each, after the dispersion had taken place. But this is improbable: first, because there is great reason to presume that Moses, who has mentioned the confusion of language, would have mentioned these circumstances also, if they had actually contributed to bring about so singular an event: secondly, because the confusion of language was sufficient of itself to have accomplished this; and we cannot suppose that the Deity could have done any thing in vain: and thirdly, because, if mankind had been dispersed, each tribe in its peculiar hue, it is impossible to conceive, that they could have wandered and settled in such a manner, as to exhibit that regular gradation of colour from the equator to the poles, so conspicuous at the present day.

These are the only periods, which there has been even the shadow of a probability for assigning; and we may therefore conclude that the preceding observations, together with such circumstances as will appear in the present chapter, will amount to a demonstration, that the difference of colour was never caused by any interposition of the Deity, and that it must have proceeded therefore from that *incidental co-operation of causes*, which has been before related.

What these causes are, it is out of the power of human wisdom positively to assert: there are facts, however, which, if properly weighed and put together, will throw considerable light upon the subject. These we shall submit to the perusal of the reader, and shall deduce from them such inferences only, as almost every person must make in his own mind, on their recital.

The first point, that occurs to be ascertained, is, "What part of the skin is the seat of colour?" The old anatomists usually divided the skin into two parts, or lamina; the exteriour and thinnest, called by the Greeks *Epidermis*, by the Romans *Cuticula*, and hence by us *Cuticle*; and the interiour, called by the former *Derma*, and by the latter *Cutis*, or *true skin*. Hence they must necessarily have supposed, that, as the *true skin* was in every respect the same in all human subjects, however various their external hue, so the seat of colour must have existed in the *Cuticle*, or upper surface.

Malphigi, an eminent Italian physician, of the last century, was the first person who discovered that the skin was divided into three lamina, or parts; the *Cuticle*, the *true skin*, and a certain coagulated substance situated between both, which he distinguished by the title of *Mucosum Corpus*; a title retained by anatomists to the present day: which coagulated substance adhered so firmly to the *Cuticle*, as, in all former anatomical preparations, to have come off with it, and, from this circumstance to have led the ancient anatomists to believe, that there were but two lamina, or divisible portions in the human skin.

This discovery was sufficient to ascertain the point in question: for it appeared afterwards that the *Cuticle*, when divided according to this discovery from the other lamina, was semi-transparent; that the cuticle of the blackest negroe was of the same transparency and colour, as that of the purest white; and hence, the *true skins* of both being invariably the same, that the *mucosum corpus* was the seat of colour.

This has been farther confirmed by all subsequent anatomical experiments, by which it appears, that, whatever is the colour of this intermediate coagulated substance, nearly the same is the apparent colour of the upper surface of the skin. Neither can it be otherwise; for the *Cuticle*, from its transparency, must necessarily transmit the colour of the substance beneath it, in the same manner, though not in the

102

same degree, as the *cornea* transmits the colour of the *iris* of the eye. This transparency is a matter of ocular demonstration in white people. It is conspicuous in every blush; for no one can imagine, that the cuticle becomes red, as often as this happens: nor is it less discoverable in the veins, which are so easy to be discerned; for no one can suppose, that the blue streaks, which he constantly sees in the fairest complexions, are painted, as it were, on the surface of the upper skin. From these, and a variety of other observations,[81] no maxim is more true in physiology, than that *on the mucosum corpus depends the colour of the human body*; or, in other words, that the *mucosum corpus* being of a different colour in different inhabitants of the globe, and appearing through the cuticle or upper surface of the skin, gives them that various appearance, which strikes us so forcibly in contemplating the human race.

As this can be incontrovertibly ascertained, it is evident, that whatever causes cooperate in producing this different appearance, they produce it by acting upon the *mucosum corpus*, which, from the almost incredible manner in which the cuticle[82] is perforated, is as accessible as the cuticle itself. These causes are probably those various qualities of things, which, combined with the influence of the sun, contribute to form what we call *climate*. For when any person considers, that the mucous substance, before-mentioned, is found to vary in its colour, as the *climates* vary from the equator to the poles, his mind must be instantly struck with the hypothesis, and he must adopt it without any hesitation, as the genuine cause of the phænomenon.

This fact,[83] *of the variation of the mucous substance according to the situation of the place*, has been clearly ascertained in the numerous anatomical experiments that have been made; in which, subjects of all nations have come under consideration. The natives of many of the kingdoms and isles of *Asia*, are found to have their *corpus mucosum* black. Those of *Africa*, situated near the line, of the same colour. Those of the maritime parts of the same continent, of a dusky brown, nearly approaching to it; and the colour becomes lighter or darker in proportion as the distance from the equator is either greater or less. The Europeans are the fairest inhabitants of the world. Those situated in the most southern regions of *Europe*, have in their *corpus mucosum* a tinge of the dark hue of their *African* neighbours: hence the epidemick complexion, prevalent among them, is nearly of the colour of the pickled Spanish olive; while in this country, and those situated nearer the north pole, it appears to be nearly, if not absolutely, white.

These are facts,[84] which anatomy has established; and we ac-knowledge them to be such, that we cannot divest ourselves of the idea, that *climate* has a considerable share in producing a difference of colour. Others, we know, have invented other hypotheses, but all of them have been instantly refuted, as unable to explain the difficulties for which they were advanced, and as absolutely contrary to fact: and the inventors themselves have been obliged, almost as soon as they have proposed them, to acknowledge them deficient.

The only objection of any consequence, that has ever been made to the hypothesis of *climate*, is this, *that people under the same parallels are not exactly of the same colour*. But this is no objection in fact: for it does not follow that those countries, which are at an equal distance from the equator, should have their climates the same. Indeed nothing is more contrary to experience than this. Climate depends upon a variety of accidents. High mountains, in the neighbourhood of a place, make it cooler, by chilling the air that is carried over them by the winds. Large spreading succulent plants, if among the productions of the soil, have the same effect: they afford agreeable cooling shades, and a moist atmosphere from their continual exhalations, by which the ardour of the sun is considerably abated. While the soil, on the other hand, if of a sandy nature, retains the heat in an uncommon degree, and makes the summers considerably hotter than those which are found to exist in the same latitude, where the soil is different. To this proximity of what may be termed *burning sands*, and to the sulphurous and metallick particles, which are continually exhaling from the bowels of the earth, is ascribed the different degree of blackness, by which some *African* nations are distinguishable from each other, though under the same parallels. To these observations we may add, that though the inhabitants of the same parallel are not exactly of the same hue, yet they differ only by shades of the same colour; or, to speak with more precision, that there are no two people, in such a situation, one of whom is white, and the other black. To sum up the whole-Suppose we were to take a common globe; to begin at the equator; to paint every country along the meridian line in succession from thence to the poles; and to paint them with the same colour which prevails in the respective inhabitants of each, we should see the black, with which we had been obliged to begin, insensibly changing to an olive, and the olive, through as many intermediate colours, to a white: and if, on the other hand, we should complete any one of the parallels according to the same plan, we should see a difference perhaps in the appearance of some of the countries through which it ran, though the difference would consist wholly in shades of the same colour.

The argument therefore, which is brought against the hypothesis, is so far from being, an objection, that we shall consider it one of the first arguments in its favour: for if *climate* has really an influence on the *mucous substance* of the body, it is evident, that we must not only expect to see a gradation of colour in the inhabitants from the equator to the poles, but also different[85] shades of the same colour in the inhabitants of the same parallel.

To this argument, we shall add one that is incontrovertible, which is, that when the *black* inhabitants of *Africa* are transplanted to *colder*, or the *white* inhabitants of *Europe* to *hotter* climates, their children, *born there*, are of a *different colour from themselves*; that is, lighter in the first, and darker in the second instance.

As a proof of the first, we shall give the words of the Abbé Raynal,[86] in his admired publication. "The children," says he, "which they, (the *Africans*) procreate in *America*, are not so black as their parents were. After each generation the difference becomes more palpable. It is possible, that after a numerous succession of generations, the men come from *Africa* would not be distinguished from those of the country, into which they may have been transplanted."

This circumstance we have had the pleasure of hearing confirmed by a variety of persons, who have been witnesses of the fact; but particularly by many intelligent[87] Africans, who have been parents themselves in *America*, and who have declared that the difference is so palpable in the *northern provinces*, that not only they themselves have constantly observed it, but that they have heard it observed by others.

Neither is this variation in the children from the colour of their parents improbable. *The children of the blackest Africans are born white.*[88] In this state they continue for about a month, when they change to a pale yellow. In process of time they become brown. Their skin still continues to increase in darkness with their age, till it becomes of a dirty, sallow black, and at length, after a certain period of years, glossy and shining. Now, if climate has any influence on the *mucous substance* of the body, this variation in the children from the colour of their parents is an event, which must be reasonably expected: for being born white, and not having equally powerful causes to act upon them in colder, as their parents had in the hotter climates which they left, it must necessarily follow, that the same affect cannot possibly be produced.

105

Hence also, if the hypothesis be admitted, may be deduced the reason, why even those children, who have been brought from their country at an early age into colder regions, have been observed[89] to be of a lighter colour than those who have remained at home till they arrived at a state of manhood. For having undergone some of the changes which we mentioned to have attended their countrymen from infancy to a certain age, and having been taken away before the rest could be completed, these farther changes, which would have taken place had they remained at home, seem either to have been checked in their progress, or weakened in their degree, by a colder climate.

We come now to the second and opposite case; for a proof of which we shall appeal to the words of Dr. Mitchell,[90] in the Philosophical Transactions. "The *Spaniards* who have inhabited *America* under the torrid zone for any time, are become as dark coloured as our native *Indians* of *Virginia*, of which, *I myself have been a witness*; and were they not to intermarry with the *Europeans*, but lead the same rude and barbarous lives with the *Indians*, it is very probable that, in a succession of many generations, they would become as dark in complexion."

To this instance we shall add one, which is mentioned by a late writer,[91] who describing the *African* coast, and the *European* settlements there, has the following passage. "There are several other small *Portuguese* settlements, and one of some note at *Mitomba*, a river in *Sierra Leon*. The people here called *Portuguese*, are principally persons bred from a mixture of the first *Portuguese discoverers* with the natives, and now become, in their *complexion* and *woolly quality* of their hair, *perfect negroes*, retaining however a smattering of the *Portuguese* language."

These facts, with respect to the colonists of the *Europeans*, are of the highest importance in the present case, and deserve a serious attention. For when we know to a certainty from whom they are descended; when we know that they were, at the time of their transplantation, of the same colour as those from whom they severally sprung; and when, on the other hand, we are credibly informed, that they have changed it for the native colour of the place which they now inhabit; the evidence in support of these facts is as great, as if a person, on the removal of two or three families into another climate, had determined to ascertain the circumstance; as if he had gone with them and watched their children; as if he had communicated his observations at his death to a successor; as if his successor had prosecuted the plan, and thus an uninterrupted chain of evidence had been kept up from their first removal to any determined period of succeeding time.

But though these facts seem sufficient of themselves to confirm our opinion, they are not the only facts which can be adduced in its support. It can be shewn, that the members of the *very same family*, when divided from each other, and removed into different countries, have not only changed their family complexion, but that they have changed it to *as many different colours* as they have gone into *different regions of the world*. We cannot have, perhaps, a more striking instance of this, than in the *Jews*. These people, are scattered over the face of the whole earth. They have preserved themselves distinct from the rest of the world by their religion; and, as they never intermarry with any but those of their own sect, so they have no mixture of blood in their veins, that they should differ from each other: and yet nothing is more true, than that the *English Jew*[92] is white, the *Portuguese* swarthy, the *Armenian* olive, and the *Arabian* copper; in short, that there appear to be as many different species of *Jews*, as there are countries in which they reside.

To these facts we shall add the following observation, that if we can give credit to the ancient historians in general, a change from the darkest black to the purest white must have actually been accomplished. One instance, perhaps, may be thought sufficient. *Herodotus*[93] relates, that the *Colchi were black*, and that they had *crisped hair*. These people were a detachment of the *Æthiopian* army under *Sesostris*, who followed him in his expedition, and settled in that part of the world, where *Colchis* is usually represented to have been situated. Had not the same author informed us of this circumstance, we should have thought it strange, [94] that a people of this description should have been found in such a latitude. Now as they were undoubtedly settled there, and as they were neither so totally destroyed, nor made any such rapid conquests, as that history should notice the event, there is great reason to presume, that their descendants continued in the same, or settled in the adjacent country; from whence it will follow, that they must have changed their complexion to that, which is observable in the inhabitants of this particular region at the present day; or, in other words, that the *black inhabitant of Colchis* must have been changed into the *fair Circassian*.[95]

As we have now shewn it to be highly probable, from the facts which have been advanced, that climate is the cause of the difference of colour which prevails in the different inhabitants of the globe, we shall now shew its probability from so similar an effect produced on the *mucous substance* before-mentioned by so similar a cause, that though the fact does not absolutely prove our conjecture to be right, yet it will give us a very lively conception of the manner, in which the phænomenon may be caused.

This probability may be shewn in the case of *freckles*, which are to be seen in the face of children, but of such only, as have the thinnest and most transparent skins, and are occasioned by the rays of the sun, striking forcibly on the *mucous substance* of the face, and drying the accumulating fluid. This accumulating fluid, or perspirable matter, is at first colourless; but being exposed to violent heat, or dried, becomes brown. Hence, the *mucosum corpus* being tinged in various parts by this brown coagulated fluid, and the parts so tinged appearing through the *cuticle*, or upper surface of the skin, arises that spotted appearance, observable in the case recited.

Now, if we were to conceive a black skin to be an *universal freckle*, or the rays of the sun to act so universally on the *mucous substance* of a person's face, as to produce these spots so contiguous to each other that they should unite, we should then see, in imagination, a face similar to those, which are daily to be seen among black people: and if we were to conceive his body to be exposed or acted upon in the same manner, we should then see his body assuming a similar appearance; and thus we should see the whole man of a perfect black, or resembling one of the naked inhabitants of the torrid zone. Now as the feat of freckles and of blackness is the same; as their appearance is similar; and as the cause of the first is the ardour of the sun, it is therefore probable that the cause of the second is the same: hence, if we substitute for the word "*sun*," what is analogous to it, the word *climate*, the same effect may be supposed to be produced, and the conjecture to receive a sanction.

Nor is it unlikely that the hypothesis, which considers the cause of freckles and of blackness as the same, may be right. For if blackness is occasioned by the rays of the sun striking forcibly and universally on the *mucous substance* of the body, and drying the accumulating fluid, we can account for the different degrees of it to be found in the different inhabitants of the globe. For as the quantity of perspirable fluid, and the force of the solar rays is successively increased, as the climates are successively warmer, from any given parallel to the line, it follows that the fluid, with which the *mucous substance* will be stained, will be successively thicker and deeper coloured; and hence, as it appears through the cuticle, the complexion successively darker;

or, what amounts to the same thing, there will be a difference of colour in the inhabitants of every successive parallel.

From these, and the whole of the preceding observations on the subject, we may conclude, that as all the inhabitants of the earth cannot be otherwise than the children of the same parents, and as the difference of their appearance must have of course proceeded from incidental causes, these causes are a combination of those qualities, which we call *climate*; that the blackness of the *Africans* is so far ingrafted in their constitution, in a course of many generations, that their children wholly inherit it, if brought up in the same spot, but that it is not so absolutely interwoven in their nature, that it cannot be removed, if they are born and settled in another; that *Noah* and his sons were probably of an *olive* complexion; that those of their descendants, who went farther to the south, became of a deeper olive or *copper*; while those, who went still farther, became of a deeper copper or *black*; that those, on the other hand, who travelled farther to the north, became less olive or *brown*, while those who went still farther than the former, became less brown or *white*; and that if any man were to point out any one of the colours which prevails in the human complexion, as likely to furnish an argument, that the people of such a complexion were of a different species from the rest, it is probable that his own descendants, if removed to the climate to which this complexion is peculiar, would, in the course of a few generations, degenerate into the same colour.

Having now replied to the argument, "that the Africans are an inferiour link of the chain of nature," as far as it depended on their *capacity* and *colour*, we shall now only take notice of an expression, which the *receivers* before-mentioned are pleased to make use of, "that they are made for slavery."

Had the Africans been *made for slavery*, or to become the property of any society of men, it is clear, from the observations that have been made in the second part of this Essay, that they must have been created *devoid of reason*: but this is contrary to fact. It is clear also, that there must have been, many and evident signs of the *inferiority of their nature*, and that this society of men must have had a *natural right* to their dominion: but this is equally false. No such signs of *inferiority* are to be found in the one, and the right to dominion in the other is *incidental*: for in what volume of nature or religion is it written, that one society of men should *breed slaves* for the benefit, of another? Nor is it less evident that they would have wanted many of those qualities which they have, and which brutes have not: they would have wanted that *spirit of liberty*, that *sense of ignominy and shame*,[96] which so frequently drives them to the horrid extremity of finishing their own existence. Nor would they have been endowed with a *contemplative power*; for such a power would have been unnecessary to people in such a situation; or rather, its only use could have been to increase their pain. We cannot suppose therefore that God has made an order of beings, with such mental qualities and powers, for the sole purpose of being used as *beasts*, or *instruments* of labour. And here, what a dreadful argument presents itself against you *receivers*? For if they have no understandings as you confess, then is your conduct impious, because, as they cannot perceive the intention of your punishment, your severities cannot make them better. But if, on the other hand, they have had understandings, (which has evidently appeared) then is your conduct equally impious, who, by destroying their faculties by the severity of your discipline, have reduced men; who had once the power of reason, to an equality with the brute creation.

Chapter 9

The reader may perhaps think, that the *receivers* have by this time expended all their arguments, but their store is not so easily exhausted. They are well aware that justice, nature, and religion, will continue, as they have ever uniformly done, to oppose their conduct. This has driven them to exert their ingenuity, and has occasioned that multiplicity of arguments to be found in the present question.

These arguments are of a different complexion from the former. They consist in comparing the state of *slaves* with that of some of the classes of *free* men, and in certain scenes of felicity, which the former are said to enjoy.

It is affirmed that the punishments which the Africans undergo, are less severe than the military; that their life is happier than that of the English peasant; that they have the advantages of manumission; that they have their little spots of ground, their holy-days, their dances; in short, that their life is a scene of festivity and mirth, and that they are much happier in the colonies than in their own country.

These representations, which have been made out with much ingenuity and art, may have had their weight with the unwary; but they will never pass with men of consideration and sense, who are accustomed to estimate the probability of things, before they admit them to be true. Indeed the bare assertion, that their situation is even comfortable, contains its own refutation, or at least leads us to suspect that the person, who asserted it, has omitted some important considerations in the account. Such we shall shew to have been actually the case, and that the representations of the *receivers*, when stripped of their glossy ornaments, are but empty declamation.

It is said, first, of *military punishments*, that they are more severe than those which the *Africans* undergo. But this is a bare assertion without a proof. It is not shewn even by those, who assert it, how the fact can be made out. We are left therefore to draw the comparison ourselves, and to fill up those important considerations, which we have just said that the *receivers* had omitted.

That military punishments are severe we confess, but we deny that they are severer than those with which they are compared. Where is the military man, whose ears have been slit, whose limbs have been mutilated, or whose eyes have been beaten out? But let us even allow, that their punishments are equal in the degree of their severity: still they must lose by comparison. The soldier is never punished but after a fair and equitable trial, and the decision of a military court; the unhappy African, at the discretion of his Lord. The one knows what particular conduct will constitute an offence;[97] the other has no such information, as he is wholly at the disposal of passion and caprice, which may impose upon any action, however laudable, the appellation of a crime. The former has it of course in his power to avoid a punishment; the latter is never safe. The former is punished for a real, the latter, often, for an imaginary fault.

Now will any person assert, on comparing the whole of those circumstances together, which relate to their respective punishments, that there can be any doubt, which of the two are in the worst situation, as to their penal systems?

With respect to the declaration, that the life of an *African* in the colonies is happier than that of an *English* peasant, it is equally false. Indeed we can scarcely withhold our indignation, when we consider, how shamefully the situation of this latter class of men has been misrepresented, to elevate the former to a state of fictitious happiness. If the representations of the *receivers* be true, it is evident that those of the most approved writers, who have placed a considerable share of happiness in the *cottage*, have been mistaken in their opinion; and that those of the rich, who have been heard to sigh, and envy the felicity of the *peasant*, have been treacherous to their own sensations.

But which are we to believe on the occasion? Those, who endeavour to dress *vice* in the habit of *virtue*, or those, who derive their opinion from their own feelings? The latter are surely to be believed; and we may conclude therefore, that the horrid picture which is given of the life of the *peasant*, has not so just a foundation as the *receivers* would, lead us to suppose. For has he no pleasure in the thought, that he lives in his *own country*, and among his relations and friends? That he is actually *free*, and that his children will be the same? That he can never be *sold* as a beast? That he can speak his mind *without the fear of the lash*? That he cannot even be struck *with impunity*? And that he partakes, equally with his superiours, of the *protection of the law*?-

112

Now, there is no one of these advantages which the *African* possesses, and no one, which the defenders of slavery take into their account.

Of the other comparisons that are usually made, we may observe in general, that, as they consist in comparing the iniquitous practice of slavery with other iniquitous practices in force among other nations, they can neither raise it to the appearance of virtue, nor extenuate its guilt. The things compared are in these instances both of them evils alike. They call equally for redress,[98] and are equally disgraceful to the governments which suffer them, if not encourage them, to exist. To attempt therefore to justify one species of iniquity by comparing it with another, is no justification at all; and is so far from answering the purpose, for which the comparison is intended, as to give us reason to suspect, that the *comparer* has but little notion either of equity or honour.

We come now to those scenes of felicity, which slaves are said to enjoy. The first advantage which they are said to experience, is that of *manumission*. But here the advocates for slavery conceal an important circumstance. They expatiate indeed on the charms of freedom, and contend that it must be a blessing in the eyes of those, upon whom it is conferred. We perfectly agree with them in this particular. But they do not tell us that these advantages are *confined*; that they are confined to some *favourite domestick*; that not *one in an hundred* enjoy them; and that they are *never* extended to those, who are employed in the *cultivation of the field*, as long as they can work. These are they, who are most to be pitied, who are destined to *perpetual* drudgery; and of whom *no one whatever* has a chance of being freed from his situation, till death either releases him at once, or age renders him incapable of continuing his former labour. And here let it be remarked, *to the disgrace of the receivers*, that he is then made free, not-*as a reward for his past services*, but, as his labour is then of little or no value,-*to save the tax*.[99]

With the same artifice is mention also made of the little spots, or *gardens*, as they are called, which slaves are said to possess from the *liberality* of *the receivers*. But people must not be led away by agreeable and pleasant sounds. They must not suppose that these gardens are made for *flowers*; or that they are places of *amusement*, in which they can spend their time in botanical researches and delights. Alas, they do not furnish them with a theme for such pleasing pursuits and speculations! They must be cultivated in those hours, which ought to be appropriated to rest;[100] and they must be cultivated, not for an amusement, but to make up, *if it be possible*, the great deficiency in their weekly allowance of provisions. Hence it appears, that the *receivers* have no merit whatever in such an appropriation of land to their unfortunate slaves: for they are either under the necessity of doing this, or of *losing* them by the jaws of famine. And it is a notorious fact, that, with their weekly allowance, and the produce of their spots together, it is often with the greatest difficulty that they preserve a wretched existence.

The third advantage which they are said to experience, is that of *holy-days*, or days of respite from their usual discipline and fatigue. This is certainly a great indulgence, and ought to be recorded to the immortal honour of the *receivers*. We wish we could express their liberality in those handsome terms, in which it deserves to be represented, or applaud them sufficiently for deviating for once from the rigours of servile discipline. But we confess, that we are unequal to the task, and must therefore content ourselves with observing, that while the horse has *one* day in *seven* to refresh his limbs, the happy *African*[101] has but *one* in *fifty-two*, as a relaxation from his labours.

With respect to their *dances*, on which such a particular stress has been generally laid, we fear that people may have been as shamefully deceived, as in the former instances. For from the manner in which these are generally mentioned, we should almost be led to imagine, that they had certain hours allowed them for the purpose of joining in the dance, and that they had every comfort and convenience, that people are generally supposed to enjoy on such convivial occasions. But this is far from the case. Reason informs us, that it can never be. If they wish for such innocent recreations, they must enjoy them in the time that is allotted them for sleep; and so far are these dances from proceeding from any uncommon degree of happiness, which excites them to convivial society, that they proceed rather from an uncommon depression of spirits, which makes them even sacrifice their rest,[102] for the sake of experiencing for a moment a more joyful oblivion of their cares. For suppose any one of the *receivers*, in the middle of a dance, were to address his slaves in the following manner: "*Africans!* I begin at last to feel for your situation; and my conscience is severely hurt, whenever I reflect that I have been reducing those to a state of misery and pain, who have never given me offence. You seem to be fond of these exercises, but yet you are obliged to take them at such unseasonable hours, that they impair your health, which is sufficiently broken by the intolerable share of labour which I have hitherto imposed upon you. I will therefore make you a proposal. Will you be content to live in the colonies, and you shall have the half of every week entirely to yourselves? or will you choose to return to your miserable, wretched country?"-But what is that which strikes their ears? Which makes them motionless in an instant? Which interrupts the festive scene?-their country?-transporting sound!-Behold! they are now flying from the dance: you may see them running to the shore, and, frantick as it were with joy, demanding with open arms an instantaneous passage to their beloved native plains.

Such are the *colonial delights*, by the representation of which the *receivers* would persuade us, that the *Africans* are taken from their country to a region of conviviality and mirth; and that like those, who leave their usual places of residence for a summer's amusement, they are conveyed to the colonies-*to bathe,-to dance,-to keep holy-day,-to be jovial*.-But there is something so truly ridiculous in the attempt to impose these scenes of felicity on the publick, as scenes which fall to the lot of slaves, that the *receivers* must have been driven to great extremities, to hazard them to the eye of censure.

The last point that remains to be considered, is the shameful assertion, that the *Africans* are much *happier in the colonies, than in their own country*. But in what does this superiour happiness consist? In those real scenes, it must be replied, which have been just mentioned; for these, by the confession of the receivers, constitute the happiness they enjoy.-But it has been shewn that these have been unfairly represented; and, were they realized in the most extensive latitude, they would not confirm the fact. For if, upon a recapitulation, it consists in the pleasure of *manumission*, they surely must have passed their lives in a much more comfortable manner, who, like the *Africans at home*, have had no occasion for such a benefit at all. But the *receivers*, we presume, reason upon this principle, that we never know the value of a blessing but by its loss. This is generally true: but would any one of them make himself a *slave* for years, that he might run the chance of the pleasures of *manumission*? Or that he might taste the charms of liberty with *a greater relish*? Nor is the assertion less false in every other consideration. For if their happiness consists in the few *holy-days*, which *in the colonies* they are permitted to enjoy, what must be their situation *in their own country*, where the whole year is but one continued holy-day, or cessation from discipline and fatigue?-If in the possession of *a mean and contracted spot*, what must be their situation, where a whole region is their own, producing almost spontaneously the comforts of life, and requiring for its cultivation none of those hours, which should be appropriated to *sleep*?-If in the pleasures of the *colonial dance*, what must it be in *their own country*, where they may dance for ever; where there is no stated hour to interrupt their felicity, no intolerable labour immediately to succeed their recreations, and no overseer to receive them under the discipline of the lash?-If these therefore are the only circumstances, by which the assertion can be proved, we may venture to say, without fear of opposition, that it can never be proved at all.

But these are not the only circumstances. It is said that they are barbarous at home.-But do you *receivers* civilize them?-Your unwillingness to convert them to Christianity, because you suppose you must use them more kindly when converted, is but a bad argument in favour of the fact.

It is affirmed again, that their manner of life, and their situation is such in their own country, that to say they are happy is a jest. "But who are you, who pretend to judge[103] of another man's happiness? That state which each man, under the guidance of his maker, forms for himself, and not one man for another? To know what constitutes mine or your happiness, is the sole prerogative of him who created us, and cast us in so various and different moulds. Did your slaves ever complain to you of their unhappiness, amidst their native woods and desarts? Or, rather, let me ask, did they ever cease complaining of their condition under you their lordly masters? Where they see, indeed, the accommodations of civil life, but see them all pass to others, themselves unbenefited by them. Be so gracious then, ye petty tyrants over human freedom, to let your slaves judge for themselves, what it is which makes their own happiness, and then see whether they do not place it *in the return to their own country*, rather than in the contemplation of your grandeur, of which their misery makes so large a part."

But since you speak with so much confidence on the subject, let us ask you *receivers* again, if you have ever been informed by your unfortunate slaves, that they had no connexions in the country from which they have forcibly been torn away: or, if you will take upon you to assert, that they never sigh, when they are alone; or that they never relate to each other their tales of misery and woe. But you judge of them, perhaps, in an happy moment, when you are dealing out to them their provisions for the week; and are but little aware, that, though the countenance may be cheered with a momentary smile, the heart may be exquisitely tortured. Were you to shew us, indeed, that there are laws, subject to no evasion, by which you are obliged to clothe and feed them in a comfortable manner; were you to shew us that they are protected[104] at all; or that even *one* in a *thousand* of those masters have suffered death,[105] who have been guilty of *premeditated* murder to their slaves, you would have a better claim to our belief: but you can neither produce the instances nor the laws. The people, of whom you speak, are *slaves*, are your own *property*, are wholly *at your own disposal*; and this idea is sufficient to overturn your assertions of their happiness.

But we shall now mention a circumstance, which, in the present case, will have more weight than all the arguments which have hitherto been advanced. It is an opinion, which the *Africans* universally entertain, that, as soon as death shall release them from the hands of their oppressors, they shall immediately be wafted back to their native plains, there to exist again, to enjoy the sight of their beloved countrymen, and to spend the whole of their new existence in scenes of tranquillity and delight; and so powerfully does this notion operate upon them, as to drive them frequently to the horrid extremity of putting a period to their lives. Now if these suicides are frequent, (which no person can deny) what are they but a proof, that the situation of those who destroy themselves must have been insupportably wretched: and if the thought of returning to their country after death, *when they have experienced the colonial joys*, constitutes their supreme felicity, what are they but a proof, that they think there is as much difference between the two situations, as there is between misery and delight?

Nor is the assertion of the *receivers* less liable to a refutation in the instance of those, who terminate their own existence, than of those, whom nature releases from their persecutions. They die with a smile upon their face, and their funerals are attended by a vast concourse of their countrymen, with every possible demonstration of joy.[106] But why this unusual mirth, if their departed brother has left an happy place? Or if he has been taken from the care of an indulgent master, who consulted his pleasures, and administered to his wants? But alas, it arises from hence, that *he is gone to his happy country*: a circumstance, sufficient of itself, to silence a myriad of those specious arguments, which the imagination has been racked, and will always be racked to produce, in favour of a system of tyranny and oppression.

It remains only, that we should now conclude the chapter with a fact, which will shew that the account, which we have given of the situation of slaves, is strictly true, and will refute at the same time all the arguments which have hitherto been, and may yet be brought by the *receivers*, to prove that their treatment is humane. In one of the western colonies of the Europeans, [107]six hundred and fifty thousand slaves were imported within an hundred years; at the expiration of which time, their whole posterity were found to amount to one hundred and forty thousand. This fact will ascertain the treatment of itself. For how shamefully must these unfortunate people have been oppressed? What a dreadful havock must famine, fatigue, and cruelty, have made among them, when we consider, that the descendants of *six hundred and fifty thousand* people in the prime of life, gradually imported within a century, are less numerous than those, which only *ten thousand*[108] would have produced in the same period, under common advantages, and in a country congenial to their constitutions?

But the *receivers* have probably great merit on the occasion. Let us therefore set it down to their humanity. Let us suppose for once, that this incredible waste of the human species proceeds from a benevolent design; that, sensible of the miseries of a servile state, they resolve to wear out, as fast as they possibly can, their unfortunate slaves, that their miseries may the sooner end, and that a wretched posterity may be prevented from sharing their parental condition. Now, whether this is the plan of reasoning which the *receivers* adopt, we cannot take upon us to decide; but true it is, that the effect produced is exactly the same, as if they had reasoned wholly on this *benevolent* principle.

Chapter 10

We have now taken a survey of the treatment which the unfortunate *Africans* undergo, when they are put into the hands of the
receivers. This treatment, by the four first chapters of the present part
of this Essay, appears to be wholly insupportable, and to be such as no
human being can apply to another, without the imputation of such
crimes, as should make him tremble. But as many arguments are usually advanced by those who have any interest in the practice, by which
they would either exculpate the treatment, or diminish its severity, we
allotted the remaining chapters for their discussion. In these we considered the probability of such a treatment against the motives of
interest; the credit that was to be given to those disinterested writers on
the subject, who have recorded particular instances of barbarity; the
inferiority of the *Africans* to the human species; the comparisons that
are generally made with respect to their situation; the positive scenes
of felicity which they are said to enjoy, and every other argument, in
short, that we have found to have ever been advanced in the defence of
slavery. These have been all considered, and we may venture to pro-
nounce, that, instead of answering the purpose for which they were
intended, they serve only to bring such circumstances to light, as
clearly shew, that if ingenuity were racked to invent a situation, that
would be the most distressing and insupportable to the human race; it
could never invent one, that would suit the description better, than the-
colonial slavery.

If this then be the case, and if slaves, notwithstanding all the arguments to the contrary, are exquisitely miserable, we ask you
receivers, by what right you reduce them to so wretched a situation?

You reply, that you *buy them*; that your *money* constitutes your
right, and that, like all other things which you purchase, they are
wholly at your own disposal.

Upon this principle alone it was, that we professed to view your
treatment, or examine your right, when we said, that "the question[109]

resolved itself into two separate parts for discussion; into the *African commerce*, as explained in the history of slavery, and the subsequent slavery in the colonies, *as founded on the equity of the commerce.*" Now, since it appears that this commerce, upon the fullest investigation, is contrary to "*the principles*[110] *of law and government, the dictates of reason, the common maxims of equity, the laws of nature, the admonitions of conscience, and, in short, the whole doctrine of natural religion,*" it is evident that the *right*, which is founded upon it, must be the same; and that if those things only are lawful in the sight of God, which are either virtuous in themselves, or proceed from virtuous principles, you *have no right over them at all.*

You yourselves also confess this. For when we ask you, whether any human being has a right to sell you, you immediately answer, No; as if nature revolted at the thought, and as if it was so contradictory to your own feelings, as not to require consideration. But who are you, that have this exclusive charter of trading in the liberties of mankind? When did nature, or rather the Author of nature, make so partial a distinction between you and them? When did He say, that you should have the privilege of selling others, and that others should not have the privilege of selling you?

Now since you confess, that no person whatever has a right to dispose of you in this manner, you must confess also, that those things are unlawful to be done to you, which are usually done in consequence of the sale. Let us suppose then, that in consequence of the *commerce* you were forced into a ship; that you were conveyed to another country; that you were sold there; that you were confined to incessant labour; that you were pinched by continual hunger and thirst; and subject to be whipped, cut, and mangled at discretion, and all this at the hands of those, whom you had never offended; would you not think that you had a right to resist their treatment? Would you not resist it with a safe conscience? And would you not be surprized, if your resistance should be termed rebellion?-By the former premises you must answer, yes.-Such then is the case with the wretched *Africans*. They have a right to resist your proceedings. They can resist them, and yet they cannot justly be considered as rebellious. For though we suppose them to have been guilty of crimes to one another; though we suppose them to have been the most abandoned and execrable of men, yet are they perfectly innocent with respect to you *receivers*. You have no right to touch even the hair of their heads without their own consent. It is not your money, that can invest you with a right. Human liberty can neither be bought nor sold. Every lash that you give them is unjust. It is a lash against nature and religion, and will surely stand recorded against you, since they are all, with respect to your *impious* selves, in a state of nature; in a state of original dissociation; perfectly free.

Chapter 11

Having now considered both the *commerce* and *slavery*, it remains only to collect such arguments as are scattered in different parts of the work, and to make such additional remarks, as present themselves on the subject.

And first, let us ask you, who have studied the law of nature, and you, who are learned in the law of the land, if all property must not be inferiour in its nature to its possessor, or, in other words, (for it is a case, which every person must bring home to his own breast) if you suppose that any human being can have *a property in yourselves*? Let us ask you appraisers, who scientifically know the value of things, if any human creature is equivalent only to any of the trinkets that you wear, or at most, to any of the horses that you ride: or in other words, if you have ever considered the most costly things that you have valued, as *equivalent to yourselves*? Let us ask you rationalists, if man, as a reasonable being, is not *accountable* for his actions, and let us put the same question to you, who have studied the divine writings? Let us ask you parents, if ever you thought that you possessed an *authority* as such, or if ever you expected a *duty* from your sons; and let us ask you sons, if ever you felt an impulse in your own breasts to *obey* your parents. Now, if you should all answer as we could wish, if you should all answer consistently with reason, nature, and the revealed voice of God, what a dreadful argument will present itself against the commerce and slavery of the human species, when we reflect, that no man whatever can be bought or reduced to the situation of a slave, *but he must instantly become a brute, he must instantly be reduced to the value of those things, which were made for his own use and convenience; he must instantly cease to be accountable for his actions, and his authority as a parent, and his duty as a son, must be instantly no more.*

Neither does it escape our notice, when we are speaking of the fatal wound which every social duty must receive, how considerably

Christianity suffers by the conduct of you *receivers*. For by prosecuting this impious commerce, you keep the *Africans* in a state of perpetual ferocity and barbarism; and by prosecuting it in such a manner, as must represent your religion, as a system of robbery and oppression, you not only oppose the propagation of the gospel, as far as you are able yourselves, but throw the most certain impediments in the way of others, who might attempt the glorious and important task.

Such also is the effect, which the subsequent slavery in the colonies must produce. For by your inhuman treatment of the unfortunate *Africans* there, you create the same insuperable impediments to a conversion. For how must they detest the very name of *Christians*, when you *Christians* are deformed by so many and dreadful vices? How must they detest that system of religion, which appears to resist the natural rights of men, and to give a sanction to brutality and murder?

But, as we are now mentioning Christianity, we must pause for a little time, to make a few remarks on the arguments which are usually deduced from thence by the *receivers*, in defence of their system of oppression. For the reader may readily suppose, that, if they did not hesitate to bring the *Old* Testament in support of their barbarities, they would hardly let the *New* escape them.

St. Paul, having converted *Onesimus* to the Christian faith, who was a fugitive slave of *Philemon*, sent him back to his master. This circumstance has furnished the *receivers* with a plea, that Christianity encourages slavery. But they have not only strained the passages which they produce in support of their assertions, but are ignorant of historical facts. The benevolent apostle, in the letter which he wrote to *Philemon*, the master of *Onesimus*, addresses him to the following effect: "I send him back to you, but not in his former capacity,[111] *not now as a servant, but above a servant, a brother beloved.* In this manner I beseech you to receive him, for though I could *enjoin* you to do it, yet I had rather it should be a matter of your *own will*, than of *necessity.*"

It appears that the same *Onesimus*, when he was sent back, was no longer *a slave*, that he was a minister of the gospel, that he was joined with *Tychicus* in an ecclesiastical commission to the church of the *Colossians*, and was afterwards bishop of *Ephesus*. If language therefore has any meaning, and if history has recorded a fact which may be believed, there is no case more opposite to the doctrine of the *receivers*, than this which they produce in its support.

It is said again, that Christianity, among the many important precepts which it contains, does not furnish us with one for the abolition of slavery. But the reason is obvious. Slavery at the time of the intro-duction of the gospel was universally prevalent, and if Christianity had abruptly declared, that the millions of slaves should have been made free, who were then in the world, it would have been universally re-jected, as containing doctrines that were dangerous, if not destructive, to society. In order therefore that it might be universally received, it never meddled, by any positive precept, with the civil institutions of the times; but though it does not expressly say, that "you shall neither buy, nor sell, nor possess a slave," it is evident that, in its general tenour, it sufficiently militates against the custom.

The first doctrine which it inculcates, is that of *brotherly love*. It commands good will towards men. It enjoins us to love our neighbours as ourselves, and to do unto all men, as we would that they should do unto us. And how can any man fulfil this scheme of universal benevo-lence, who reduces an unfortunate person *against his will*, to the *most insupportable* of all human conditions; who considers him as his *pri-vate property*, and treats him, not as a brother, nor as one of the same parentage with himself, but as an *animal of the brute creation?*

But the most important doctrine is that, by which we are assured that mankind are to exist in a future state, and to give an account of those actions, which they have severally done in the flesh. This strikes at the very root of slavery. For how can any man be justly called to an account for his actions, whose actions are not *at his own disposal?* This is the case with the *proper*[112] slave. His liberty is absolutely bought and *appropriated*; and if the purchase is *just and equitable*, he is *under the necessity* of perpetrating any crime, which the purchaser may order him to commit, or, in other words, of ceasing to be *ac-countable for his actions*.

These doctrines therefore are sufficient to shew, that slavery is incompatible, with the Christian system. The *Europeans* considered them as such, when, at the close of the twelfth century, they resisted, their hereditary prejudices, and occasioned its abolition. Hence one, among many other proofs, that Christianity was the production of infi-nite wisdom; that though it did not take such express cognizance of the wicked national institutions of the times, as should hinder its recep-tion, it should yet contain such doctrines, as, when it should be fully established, would be sufficient for the abolition of them all.

Thus then is the argument of you *receivers* ineffectual, and your conduct impious. For, by the prosecution of this wicked slavery and commerce, you not only oppose the propagation of that gospel which was ordered to be preached unto every creature, and bring it into contempt, but you oppose its tenets also: first, because you violate that law of *universal benevolence*, which was to take away those hateful distinctions of *Jew* and *Gentile, Greek* and *Barbarian, bond* and *free*, which prevailed when the gospel was introduced; and secondly, because, as every man is to give an account of his actions hereafter, it is necessary that he should be *free*.

Another argument yet remains, which, though nature will absolutely turn pale at the recital, cannot possibly be omitted. In those wars, which are made for the sake of procuring slaves, it is evident that the contest must be generally obstinate, and that great numbers must be slain on both sides, before the event can be determined. This we may reasonably apprehend to be the case: and we have shewn,[113] that there have not been wanting instances, where the conquerors have been so incensed at the resistance they have found, that their spirit of vengeance has entirely got the better of their avarice, and they have murdered, in cool blood, every individual, without discrimination, either of age or sex. From these and other circumstances, we thought we had sufficient reason to conclude, that, where *ten* were supposed to be taken, an *hundred*, including the victors and vanquished, might be supposed to perish. Now, as the annual exportation from *Africa* consists of an hundred thousand men, and as the two orders, of those who are privately kidnapped by individuals, and of those, who are publickly seized by virtue of the authority of their prince, compose together, at least, nine-tenths of the *African* slaves, it follows, that about ten thousand consist of convicts and prisoners of war. The last order is the most numerous. Let us suppose then that only six thousand of this order are annually sent into servitude, and it will immediately appear that no less than *sixty-thousand* people annually perish in those wars, which are made only for the purpose of procuring slaves. But that this number, which we believe to be by no means exaggerated, may be free from all objection, we will include those in the estimate, who die as they are travelling to the ships. Many of these unfortunate people have a journey of one thousand miles to perform on foot, and are driven like sheep through inhospitable woods and deserts, where they frequently die in great numbers, from fatigue and want. Now if to those, who thus perish on the *African* continent, by war and travelling, we subjoin those,[114] who afterwards perish on the voyage, and in the seasoning together, it will appear that, in every yearly attempt to supply the colonies, an *hundred thousand* must perish, even before *one* useful individual can be obtained.

Gracious God! how wicked, how beyond all example impious, must be that servitude, which cannot be carried on without the continual murder of so many and innocent persons! What punishment is not to be expected for such monstrous and unparalleled barbarities! For if the blood of one man, unjustly shed, cries with so loud a voice for the divine vengeance, how shall the cries and groans of an *hundred thousand* men, *annually murdered*, ascend the celestial mansions, and bring down that punishment, which such enormities deserve! But do we mention punishment? Do we allude to that punishment, which shall be inflicted on men as individuals, in a future life? Do we allude to that awful day, which shall surely come, when the master shall behold his murdered negroe face to face? When a train of mutilated slaves shall be brought against him? When he shall stand confounded and abashed? Or, do we allude to that punishment, which may be inflicted on them here, as members of a wicked community? For as a body politick, if its members are ever so numerous, may be considered as an whole, acting of itself, and by itself, in all affairs in which it is concerned, so it is accountable, as such, for its conduct; and as these kinds of polities have only their existence here, so it is only in this world, that, as such, they can be punished.

"Now, whether we consider the crime, with respect to the individuals immediately concerned in this most barbarous and cruel traffick, or whether we consider it as patronized[115] and encouraged by the laws of the land, it presents to our view an equal degree of enormity. A crime, founded on a dreadful pre-eminence in wickedness,-a crime, which being both of individuals and the nation, must sometime draw down upon us the heaviest judgment of Almighty God, who made of one blood all the sons of men, and who gave to all equally a natural right to liberty; and who, ruling all the kingdoms of the earth with equal providential justice, cannot suffer such deliberate, such monstrous iniquity, to pass long unpunished."[116]

But alas! he seems already to have interfered on the occasion! The violent[117] and supernatural agitations of all the elements, which, for a series of years, have prevailed in those European settlements, where the unfortunate *Africans* are retained in a state of slavery, and which have brought unspeakable calamities on the inhabitants, and publick losses on the states to which they severally belong, are so many awful visitations of God for this inhuman violation of his laws. And it is not perhaps unworthy of remark, that as the subjects of Great-Britain have two thirds of this impious commerce in their own hands, so they have suffered[118] in the same proportion, or more severely than the rest.

How far these misfortunes may appear to be acts of providence, and to create an alarm to those who have been accustomed to refer every effect to its apparent cause; who have been habituated to stop there, and to overlook the finger of God; because it is slightly covered under the veil of secondary laws, we will not pretend to determine? but this we will assert with confidence, that the *Europeans* have richly deserved them all; that the fear of sympathy, which can hardly be restrained on other melancholy occasions, seems to forget to flow at the relation of these; and that we can never, with any shadow of justice, with prosperity to the undertakers of those, whose success must be at the expence of the happiness of millions of their fellow-creatures.

But this is sufficient. For if liberty is only an adventitious right; if men are by no means superiour to brutes; if every social duty is a curse; if cruelty is highly to be esteemed; if murder is strictly honourable, and Christianity is a lye; then it is evident, that the *African* slavery may be pursued, without either the remorse of conscience, or the imputation of a crime. But if the contrary of this is true, which reason must immediately evince, it is evident that no custom established among men was ever more impious; since it is contrary to *reason, justice, nature, the principles of law and government, the whole doctrine, in short, of natural religion, and the revealed voice of God.*

Endnotes

1 A Description of Guinea, with an Inquiry into the Rise and Progress of the Slave Trade, &c.-A Caution to Great Britain and her Colonies, in a short Representation of the calamitous State of the enslaved Negroes in the British Dominions. Besides several smaller pieces.

2 They had censured the *African Trade* in the year 1727, but had taken no publick notice of the *colonial* slavery till this time.

3 The instance of the *Dutch* colonists at the Cape, in the first part of the Essay; the description of an African battle, in the second; and the poetry of a negroe girl in the third, are the only considerable additions that have been made.

4 Genesis, Ch. 47. Leviticus XXV. v. 39, 40.

5 The *Thetes* appear very early in the Grecian History.--kai tines auto kouroi epont'Ithakes exairetoi; he eoi autou thentes te Dmoes(?) te; Od. Homer. D. 642. They were afterwards so much in use that, "Murioi depou apedidonto eautous ose douleuein kata sungraphen," till Solon suppressed the custom in Athens.

6 The mention of these is frequent among the classics; they were called in general *mercenarii*, from the circumstances of their *hire*, as "quibus, non malè præcipiunt, qui ita jubent uti, ut *mercenariis*, operam exigendam, justa proebenda. Cicero de off." But they are sometimes mentioned in the law books by the name of *liberi*, from the circumstances of their *birth*, to distinguish them from the *alieni*, or foreigners, as Justinian. D. 7. 8. 4.-Id. 21. 1. 25. &c. &c. &c.

7 "Nomos en pasin anthropois aidios esin, otan polemounton polis alo, ton elonton einai kai ta somata ton en te poleis, kai ta chremata." Xenoph. Kyrou Paid. L. 7. fin.

8 "Proud Nimrod first the bloody chace began,
A mighty hunter, and his prey was man."
-POPE.
9 Thucydides. L. 1. sub initio.
10 Idem.-"the strongest," says he, "engaging in these adventures,
Kerdous tou spheterou auton eneka kai tois asthenesi trophes."
11 Homer. Odyss. L. 15. 385.
12 Xenoph. Kyrou Anab. L. 6. sub initio.
13 ouk echontos po Aischynen toutou tou ergou pherontos de ti
kai   Doxes   mallon.   Thucydides,   L.   1.   sub   initio.
kai   euklees   touto   oi   Kilikes   enomizon.   Sextus   Empiricus.
ouk adoxon all'endoxon touto. Schol. &c. &c.
14 Aristoph. Plut. Act. 2. Scene 5.
15 Zenoph. Apomnemon, L. 1.
16 Herodotus. L. 2. 113.
17 "Apud Ægyptios, si quis servum sponte occiderat, eum
morte damnari æque ac si liberum occidisset, jubebant leges &c."
Diodorus Sic. L. 1.
18 "Atq id ne vos miremini, Homines servulos
Potare, amare, atq ad coenam condicere.
Licet hoc Athenis.
Plautus. Sticho."
19 "Be me kratison esin eis to Theseion
Dramein, ekei d'eos an eurombou prasin
menein" Aristoph. Horæ.

Kaka toiade paskousin oude prasin
Aitousin. Eupolis. poleis.
20 To this privilege Plautus alludes in his *Casina*, where he intro-
duces a slave, speaking in the following manner.
"Quid tu me verò libertate territas?
Quod si tu nolis, siliusque etiam tuus
Vobis *invitis*, atq amborum *ingratiis*,
Una libella liber possum fieri."
21 Homer. Odys. P. 322. In the latest edition of Homer, the word,
which we have translated *senses*, is *Aretae*, or *virtue*, but the old and
proper reading is *Noos*, as appears from Plato de Legibus, ch. 6, where
he quotes it on a similar occasion.
22 Aristotle. Polit. Ch. 2. et inseq.

23 Ellesin hegemonikos, tois de Barbarois despotikos krasthar kai ton men os philon kai oikeion epimeleisthai, tois de os zoois he phytois prospheresthai. Plutarch. de Fortun. Alexand. Orat. 1.

24 Omne tulit punctum, qui miscuit utile dulci. Horace.

25 me tacha pikren Aigypton kai Kypron idnai. Hom. Odyss. L. 17. 448.

26 L. 26.

27 Exodus. Ch. 1.

28 Vide note 1st. (Here shown as footnote 25).

29 This strikes us the more forcibly, as it is stiled *eurreiten* and *perikallea*, "*beautiful and well watered*," in all other passages where it is mentioned, but this.

30 The following short history of the African servitude, is taken from Astley's Collection of Voyages, and from the united testimonies of Smyth, Adanson, Bosman, Moore, and others, who were agents to the different factories established there; who resided many years in the country; and published their respective histories at their return. These writers, if they are partial at all, may be considered as favourable rather to their own countrymen, than the unfortunate Africans.

31 We would not wish to be understood, that slavery was unknown in Africa before the *piratical* expeditions of the *Portuguese*, as it appears from the *Nubian's Geography*, that both the slavery and commerce had been established among the natives with one another. We mean only to assert, that the *Portuguese* were the first of the *Europeans*, who made their *piratical* expeditions, and shewed the way to that *slavery*, which now makes so disgraceful a figure in the western colonies of the *Europeans*. In the term "Europeans," wherever it shall occur in the remaining part of this first dissertation, we include the *Portuguese*, and *those nations only*, who followed their example.

32 The *Portuguese* erected their first fort at *D'Elmina*, in the year 1481, about forty years after Alonzo Gonzales had pointed the Southern Africans out to his countrymen as articles of commerce.

33 In the ancient servitude, we reckoned *convicts* among the *voluntary* slaves, because they had it in their power, by a virtuous conduct, to have avoided so melancholy a situation; in the *African*, we include them in the *involuntary*, because, as virtues are frequently construed into crimes, from the venal motives of the traffick, no person whatever possesses such a *power* or *choice*.

34 Andrew Sparrman, M.D. professor of Physick at Stockholm, fellow of the Royal Academy of Sciences in Sweden, and inspector of

its cabinet of natural history, whose voyage was translated into English, and published in 1785.

35 Boshies-man, or *wild Hottentot.*

36 This conclusion concerning the dissociated state of mankind, is confirmed by all the early writers, with whose descriptions of primitive times no other conclusion is reconcileable.

37 Justin. L. 2. C. 2.

38 Sallust. Bell. Jug.

39 Sallust. Bell. Catil.

40 Ammianus Marcellinus. L. 31. C. 2. et. inseq.

41 Agri pro Numero Cultorum ab universis per vicos occupantur, quos mox inter se secundum dignationem partiuntur. Tacitus. C. 26. de Mor. Germ.

42 The author has lately read a work, intitled Paley's Moral and Political Philosophy, which, in this one respect, favours those which have been hinted at, as it denies that government was a contract. "No social compact was ever made in fact,"-"it is to suppose it possible to call savages out of caves and deserts, to deliberate upon topicks, which the experience and studies, and the refinements of civil life alone suggest. Therefore no government in the universe begun from this original." But there are no grounds for so absurd a supposition; for government, and of course the social compact, does not appear to have been introduced at the time, when families coming out of their caves and deserts, or, in other words, quitting their former *dissociated* state, joined themselves together. They had lived a considerable time in *society*, like the Lybians and Gætulians before-mentioned, and had felt many of the disadvantages of a want of discipline and laws, before government was introduced at all. The author of this Essay, before he took into consideration the origin of government, was determined, in a matter of such importance, to be biassed by no opinion whatever, and much less to indulge himself in speculation. He was determined solely to adhere to fact, and, by looking into the accounts left us of those governments which were in their infancy, and, of course in the least complicated state, to attempt to discover their foundation: he cannot say therefore, that upon a very minute perusal of the excellent work before quoted, he has been so far convinced, as to retract in the least from his sentiments on this head, and to give up maxims, which are drawn from historical facts, for those, which are the result of speculation. He may observe here, that whether government was a *contract* or not, it will not affect the reasoning of the present Essay; since where ever the contract is afterwards mentioned, it is inferred only that its

object was "the *happiness of the people*," which is confessedly the end of government. Notwithstanding this, he is under the necessity of inserting this little note, though he almost feels himself ungrateful in contradicting a work, which has afforded him so much entertainment.

43 *Jure Gentium* servi nostri sunt, qui ab hostibus capiuntur. Justinian, L. 1. 5. 5. 1.

44 *Serverum* appellatio ex eo fluxit, quod imperatores nostri captivos vendere, ac per hoc *servare*, nec occidere solent.

45 Nam sive victoribus *jure captivitatis* servissent, &c. Justin, L. 4. 3. et passim apud scriptores antiquos.

46 Neque est contra naturam spoliare eum, si possis, quem honestum est necare. Cicero de officiis. L. 3. 6.

47 1. Ut liberi suis legibus viverent. Livy, L. 30. 37.

2. Decem millia talentum argenti descripta pensionibus æquis in annos quinquaginta solverent. Ibid.

3. Et naves rostratas, præter decem triremes, traderent, elephantosque, quos haberent domitos; neque domarent alios; Bellum neve in Africa, neve extra Africam, injussu P. R. gererent, &c. Ibid.

48 The total annual exportation from Africa, is estimated here at 100,000 men, two thirds of whom are exported by the British merchants alone. This estimate is less than that which is usually made, and has been published. The author has been informed by disinterested people, who were in most of the West India islands during the late war, and who conversed with many of the most intelligent of the negroes, for the purpose of inquiring by what methods they had originally been reduced to slavery, that they did not find even two in twenty, who had been reduced to that situation, by any other means than those mentioned above. The author, desirous of a farther confirmation of this circumstance, stopped the press till he had written to another friend, who had resided twenty years in the West-Indies, and whose opinion he had not yet asked. The following is an extract from the answer. "I do not among many hundreds recollect to have seen but one or two slaves, of those imported from Africa, who had any scars to shew, that they had been in war. They are generally such as are kidnapped, or sold by their tyrants, after the destruction of a village. In short, I am firmly of opinion, that crimes and war together do not furnish one slave in an hundred of the numbers introduced into the European colonies. Of consequence the trade itself, were it possible to suppose convicts or prisoners of war to be justly sentenced to servitude, is accountable for ninety-nine in every hundred slaves, whom it

supplies. It an insult to the publick, to attempt to palliate the method of procuring them."

49 The writer of the letter of which this is a faithful extract, and who was known to the author of the present Essay, was a long time on the African coast. He had once the misfortune to be shipwrecked there, and to be taken by the natives, who conveyed him and his companions a considerable way up into the country. The hardships which he underwent in the march, his treatment during his captivity, the scenes to which he was witness, while he resided among the inland Africans, as well as while in the African trade, gave occasion to a series of very interesting letters. These letters were sent to the author of the present Essay, with liberty to make what use of them he chose, by the gentleman to whom they were written.

50 Were this not the case, the government of a country could have no right to take cognizance of crimes, and punish them, but every individual, if injured, would have a right to punish the aggressor with his own hand, which is contrary to the notions of all civilized men, whether among the ancients or the moderns.

51 This same notion is entertained even by the African princes, who do not permit the person injured to revenge his injury, or to receive the convict as his slave. But if the very person who has been *injured*, does not possess him, much less ought any other person whatsoever.

52 There are instances on the African continent, of *parents* selling their *children*. As the slaves of this description are so few, and are so irregularly obtained, we did not think it worth our while to consider them as forming an order; and, as God never gave the parent a power over his child to make him *miserable*, we trust that any farther mention of them will be unnecessary.

53 Abbè Raynal, Hist. Phil. vol. 4. P. 154.

54 Justin, L. 2. C. 1.

55 Cicero de Officiis. L. 1. C. 8.

56 It is universally allowed, that at least one fifth of the exported negroes perish in the passage. This estimate is made from the time in which they are put on board, to the time when they are disposed of in the colonies. The French are supposed to lose the greatest number in the voyage, but particularly from this circumstance, because their slave ships are in general so very large, that many of the slaves that have been put on board sickly, die before the cargo can be completed.

57 This instance happened in a ship, commanded by one Collingwood. On the 29th of November, 1781, fifty-four of them were thrown

into the sea alive; on the 30th forty-two more; and in about three days afterwards, twenty-six. Ten others, who were brought upon the deck for the same purpose, did not wait to be hand-cuffed, but bravely leaped into the sea, and shared the fate of their companions. It is a fact, that the people on board this ship had not been put upon short allowance. The excuse which this execrable wretch made on board for his conduct, was the following, "*that if the slaves, who were then sickly, had died a natural death, the loss would have been the owners; but as they were thrown alive into the sea, it would fall upon the underwriters.*"

58 This gentleman is at present resident in England. The author of this Essay applied to him for some information on the treatment of slaves, so far as his own knowledge was concerned. He was so obliging as to furnish him with the written account alluded to, interspersed only with such instances, as he himself could undertake to answer for. The author, as he has never met with these instances before, and as they are of such high authority, intends to transcribe two or three of them, and insert them in the fourth chapter. They will be found in inverted commas.

59 One third of the whole number imported, is often computed to be lost in the seasoning, which, in round numbers, will be 27000. The loss in the seasoning depends, in a great measure, on two circumstances, viz. on the number of what are called refuse slaves that are imported, and on the quantity of new land in the colony. In the French windward islands of Martinico, and Guadaloupe, which are cleared and highly cultivated, and in our old small islands, one fourth, including refuse slaves, is considered as a general proportion. But in St. Domingo, where there is a great deal of new land annually taken into culture, and in other colonies in the same situation, the general proportion, including refuse slaves, is found to be one third. This therefore is a lower estimate than the former, and reduces the number to about 23000. We may observe, that this is the common estimate, but we have reduced it to 20000 to make it free from all objection.

60 Including the number that perish on the voyage, and in the seasoning. It is generally thought that not half the number purchased can be considered as an additional stock, and of course that 50,000 are consumed within the first two years from their embarkation.

61 That part of the account, that has been hitherto given, extends to all the Europeans and their colonists, who are concerned in this horrid practice. But we are sorry that we must now make a distinction, and confine the remaining part, of it to the colonists of the British

West India islands, and to those of the southern provinces of North America. As the employment of slaves is different in the two parts of the world last mentioned, we shall content ourselves with describing it, as it exists in one of them, and we shall afterwards annex such treatment and such consequences as are applicable to both. We have only to add, that the reader must not consider our account as *universally*, but only generally, true.

62 This computation is made on a supposition, that the gang is divided into three bodies; we call it therefore moderate, because the gang is frequently divided into two bodies, which must therefore set up alternately *every other night*.

63 An hand or arm being frequently ground off.

64 The reader will scarcely believe it, but it is a fact, that a slave's annual allowance from his master, for provisions, clothing, medicines when sick, &c. is limited, upon an average, to thirty shillings.

65 "A boy having received six slaves as a present from his father, immediately slit their ears, and for the following reason, that as his father was a whimsical man, he might claim them again, unless they were marked." We do not mention this instance as a confirmation of the passage to which it is annexed, but only to shew, how cautious we ought to be in giving credit to what may be advanced in any work written in defence of slavery, by any native of the colonies: for being trained up to scenes of cruelty from his cradle, he may, consistently with his own feelings, represent that treatment as mild, at which we, who have never been used to see them, should absolutely shudder.

66 In this case he is considered as a criminal against the state. The *marshal*, an officer answering to our sheriff, superintends his execution, and the master receives the value of the slave from the publick treasury. We may observe here, that in all cases where the delinquent is a criminal of the state, he is executed, and his value is received in the same manner; He is tried and condemned by two or three justices of the peace, and without any intervention of a *jury*.

67 Particularly in Jamaica. These observations were made by disinterested people, who were there for three or four years during the late war.

68 The action was brought by the owners against the underwriters, to recover the value of the *murdered* slaves. It was tried at Guildhall.

69 Phillis Wheatley, negro slave to Mr. John Wheatley, of Boston, in New-England.

70 Lest it should be doubted whether these Poems are genuine, we shall transcribe the names of those, who signed a certificate of their authenticity.
His Excellency Thomas Hutchinson, Governor.
The Honourable Andrew Oliver, Lieutenant Governor.
The Hon. Thomas Hubbard
The Hon. John Erving
The Hon. James Pitts
The Hon. Harrison Gray
The Hon. James Bowdoin
John Hancock, Esq.
Joseph Green, Esq.
Richard Carey, Esq.
The Rev. Cha. Chauncy, D.D.
The Rev. Mather Byles, D.D.
The Rev. Ed. Pemberton, D.D.
The Rev. Andrew Elliot, D.D.
The Rev. Sam. Cooper, D.D.
The Rev. Samuel Mather
The Rev. John Moorhead
Mr. John Wheatley, her Master.

71 In the Preface.

72 As to Mr. Hume's assertions with respect to African capacity, we have passed them over in silence, as they have been so admirably refuted by the learned Dr. Beattie, in his Essay on Truth, to which we refer the reader. The whole of this admirable refutation extends from p. 458. to 464.

73 Genesis, ch. iv. 15.

74 Genesis, ch. ix. 25, 26, 27.

75 Jeremiah says, ch. xiii. 23, "Can the Æthiopian change his colour, or the leopard his spots?" Now the word, which is here translated *Æthiopian*, is in the original Hebrew "*the descendant of Cush*," which shews that this colour was not confined to the descendants of *Canaan*, as the advocates for slavery assert.

76 It is very extraordinary that the advocates for slavery should consider those Africans, whom they call negroes, as the descendants of *Canaan*, when few historical facts can be so well ascertained, as that out of the descendants of the four sons of Ham, the descendants of Canaan were the only people, (if we except the Carthaginians, who were a colony of Canaan, and were afterwards ruined) who did not settle in that quarter of the globe. Africa was incontrovertibly peopled by the

posterity of the three other sons. We cannot shew this in a clearer manner, than in the words of the learned Mr. Bryant, in his letter to Mr. Granville Sharp on this subject.

"We learn from scripture, that Ham had four sons, *Chus, Mizraim, Phut*, and *Canaan*, Gen. x. 5, 6. *Canaan* occupied *Palestine*, and the country called by his name: *Mizraim, Egypt*: but *Phut* passed deep into *Africa*, and, I believe, most of the nations in that part of the world are descended from him; at least more than from any other person." *Josephus* says, "*that Phut was the founder of the nations in Libya, and the people were from him called (phoutoi) Phuti.*" Antiq. L. 1. c. 7. "By *Lybia* he understands, as the *Greeks* did, *Africa* in general: for the particular country called *Lybia Proper*, was peopled by the *Lubim*, or *Lehabim*, one of the branches from *Mizraim*, (Labieim ex ou Libnes) Chron. Paschale, p. 29.

The sons of *Phut* settled in *Mauritania*, where was a country called *Phutia*, and a river of the like denomination. Mauritaniæ Fluvius usque ad præsens Tempus *Phut* dicitur, omnisq; circa eum Regio *Phutensis*. Hieron. Tradit. Hebroeæ.-Amnem, quem vocant *Fut*." Pliny, L. 5. c. 1. Some of this family settled above Ægypt, near Æthiopia, and were styled Troglodytæ. (phoud ex ou troglodotai.) Syncellus, p. 47. Many of them passed inland, and peopled the Mediterranean country."

"In process of time the sons of *Chus* also, (after their expulsion from Egypt) made settlements upon the sea coast of *Africa*, and came into *Mauritania*. Hence we find traces of them also in the names of places, such as *Churis, Chusares*, upon the coast: and a river *Chusa*, and a city *Cotta*, together with a promontory, *Cotis*, in *Mauritania*, all denominated from *Chus*; who at different times, and by different people, was called *Chus, Cuth, Cosh*, and *Cotis*. The river *Cusa* is mentioned by *Pliny*, Lib. 5. c. 1. and by *Ptolomy*."

"Many ages after these settlements, there was another eruption of the *Cushites* into these parts, under the name of *Saracens* and *Moors*, who over-ran *Africa*, to the very extremity of Mount Atlas. They passed over and conquered *Spain* to the north, and they extended themselves southward, as I said in my treatise, to the rivers *Senegal* and *Gambia*, and as low as the *Gold Coast*. I mentioned this, because I do not think that they proceeded much farther: most of the nations to the *south* being, as I imagine, of the race of *Phut*. The very country upon the river *Gambia* on one side, is at this day called *Phuta*, of which *Bluet*, in his history of *Juba Ben Solomon*, gives an account."

77 When America was first discovered, it was thought by some, that the scripture account of the creation was false, and that there were different species of men, because they could never suppose that people, in so rude a state as the Americans, could have transported themselves to that continent from any parts of the known world. This opinion however was refuted by the celebrated Captain Cooke, who shewed that the traject between the continents of Asia and America, was as short as some, which people in as rude a state have been actually known to pass. This affords an excellent caution against an ill-judged and hasty censure of the divine writings, because every difficulty which may be started, cannot be instantly cleared up.

78 The divine writings, which assert that all men were derived from the *same stock*, shew also, in the same instance of *Cush*, (Footnote 75), that some of them had changed their original complexion.

79 The following are the grand colours discernible in mankind, between which there are many shades;

White
Copper
Olive
Brown
Black

80 See note, (Footnote 75). To this we may add, that the rest of the descendants of *Ham*, as far as they can be traced, are now also black, at well as many of the descendants of *Shem*.

81 Diseases have a great effect upon the *mucosum corpus*, but particularly the jaundice, which turns it yellow. Hence, being transmitted through the cuticle, the yellow appearance of the whole body. But this, even as a matter of ocular demonstration, is not confined solely to white people; negroes themselves, while affected with these or other disorders, changing their black colour for that which the disease has conveyed to the *mucous* substance.

82 The cutaneous pores are so excessively small, that one grain of sand, (according to Dr. Lewenhoeck's calculations) would cover many hundreds of them.

83 We do not mean to insinuate that the same people have their *corpus mucosum* sensibly vary, as often as they go into another latitude, but that the fact is true only of different people, who have been long established in different latitudes.

84 We beg leave to return our thanks here to a gentleman, eminent in the medical line, who furnished us with the above-mentioned facts.

85 Suppose we were to see two nations, contiguous to each other, of black and white inhabitants in the same parallel, even this would be no objection, for many circumstances are to be considered. A black people may have wandered into a white, and a white people into a black latitude, and they may not have been settled there a sufficient length of time for such a change to have been accomplished in their complexion, as that they should be like the old established inhabitants of the parallel, into which they have lately come.

86 Justamond's Abbe Raynal, v. 5. p. 193.

87 The author of this Essay made it his business to inquire of the most intelligent of those, whom he could meet with in London, as to the authenticity of the fact. All those from *America* assured him that it was strictly true; those from the West-Indies, that they had never observed it there; but that they had found a sensible difference in themselves since they came to England.

88 This circumstance, which always happens, shews that they are descended from the same parents as ourselves; for had they been a distinct species of men, and the blackness entirely ingrafted in their constitution and frame, there is great reason to presume, that their children would have been born *black*.

89 This observation was communicated to us by the gentleman in the medical line, to whom we returned our thanks for certain anatomical facts.

90 Philos. Trans. No. 476. sect. 4.

91 Treatise upon the Trade from Great Britain to Africa, by an African merchant.

92 We mean such only as are *natives* of the countries which we mention, and whose ancestors have been settled there for a certain period of time.

93 Herodotus. Euterpe. p. 80. Editio Stephani, printed 1570.

94 This circumstance confirms what we said in a former note, (Footnote 85), that even if two nations were to be found in the same parallel, one of whom was black, and the other white, it would form no objection against the hypothesis of climate, as one of them might have been new settlers from a distant country.

95 Suppose, without the knowledge of any historian, they had made such considerable conquests, as to have settled themselves at the distance of 1000 miles in any one direction from *Colchis*, still they must have changed their colour. For had they gone in an Eastern or Western direction, they must have been of the same colour as the *Cir-*

cassians; if to the north, whiter; if to the south, of a copper. There are no people within that distance of *Colchis*, who are black.

96 There are a particular people among those transported from Africa to the colonies, who immediately on receiving punishment, destroy themselves. This is a fact which the *receivers* are unable to contradict.

97 The articles of war are frequently read at the head of every regiment in the service, stating those particular actions which are to be considered as crimes.

98 We cannot omit here to mention one of the customs, which has been often brought as a palliation of slavery, and which prevailed but a little time ago, and we are doubtful whether it does not prevail now, in the metropolis of this country, of kidnapping men for the service of the East-India Company. Every subject, as long as he behaves well, has a right to the protection of government; and the tacit permission of such a scene of iniquity, when it becomes known, is as much a breach of duty in government, as the conduct of those subjects, who, on other occasions, would be termed, and punished as, rebellious.

99 The expences of every parish are defrayed by a poll-tax on negroes, to save which they pretend to liberate those who are past labour; but they still keep them employed in repairing fences, or in doing some trifling work on a scanty allowance. For to free a *field-negroe*, so long as he can work, is a maxim, which, notwithstanding the numerous boasted manumissions, no master *ever thinks of adopting* in the colonies.

100 They must be cultivated always on a *Sunday*, and frequently in those hours which should be appropriated to *sleep*, or the wretched possessors must be inevitably *starved*.

101 They are allowed in general three holy-days at Christmas, but in Jamaica they have two also at Easter, and two at Whitsuntide: so that on the largest scale, they have only seven days in a year, or one day in fifty-two. But this is on a supposition, that the receivers do not break in upon the afternoons, which they are frequently too apt to do. If it should be said that Sunday is an holy-day, it is not true; it is so far an holy-day, that they do not work for their masters; but such an holy-day, that if they do not employ it in the cultivation of their little spots, they must *starved*.

102 These dances are usually in the middle of the night; and so desirous are these unfortunate people of obtaining but a joyful hour, that they not only often give up their sleep, but add to the labours of the day, by going several miles to obtain it.

103 Bishop of Glocester's sermon, preached before the society for the propagation of the gospel, at the anniversary meeting, on the 21st of February, 1766.

104 There is a law, (but let the reader remark, that it prevails but in *one* of the colonies), against mutilation. It took its rise from the frequency of the inhuman practice. But though a master cannot there chop off the limb of a slave with an axe, he may yet work, starve, and beat him to death with impunity.

105 *Two* instances are recorded by the *receivers*, out of about *fifty-thousand*, where a white man has suffered death for the murder of a negroe; but the receivers do not tell us, that these suffered more because they were the pests of society, than because the *murder of slaves was a crime*.

106 A negroe-funeral is considered as a curious sight, and is attended with singing, dancing, musick, and every circumstance that can shew the attendants to be happy on the occasion.

107 In 96 years, ending in 1774, 800,000 slaves had been imported into the French part of St. Domingo, of which there remained only 290,000 in 1774. Of this last number only 140,000 were creoles, or natives of the island, i. e. of 650,000 slaves, the whole posterity were 140,000. *Considerations sur la Colonie de St. Dominique,*(See errata-should be read as "*St. Domingue*") published by authority in 1777.

108 Ten thousand people under fair advantages, and in a soil congenial to their constitutions, and where the means of subsistence are easy, should produce in a century 160,000. This is the proportion in which the Americans increased; and the Africans in their own country increase in the same, if not in a greater proportion. Now as the climate of the colonies is as favourable to their health as that of their own country, the causes of the prodigious decrease in the one, and increase in the other, will be more conspicuous.

109 See Part II Chapter I second paragraph.

110 See Part II Chapter IX last paragraph.

111 Epist. to Philemon.

112 The *African* slave is of this description; and we could wish, in all our arguments on the present subject, to be understood as having spoken only of *proper slaves*. The slave who is condemned to the oar, to the fortifications, and other publick works, is in a different predicament. His liberty is not *appropriated*, and therefore none of those consequences can be justly drawn, which have been deduced in the present case.

113 See the description of an African battle (Footnote 49).

114 The lowest computation is 40,000, (Footnote 60).

115 The legislature has squandered away more money in the prosecution of the slave trade, within twenty years, than in any other trade whatever, having granted from the year 1750, to the year 1770, the sum of 300,000 pounds.

116 Sermon preached before the University of Cambridge, by the Rev. Peter Peckard.

117 The first noted earthquake at Jamaica, happened June the 7th 1692, when Port Royal was totally sunk. This was succeeded by one in the year 1697, and by another in the year 1722, from which time to the present, these regions of the globe seem to have been severely visited, but particularly during the last six or seven years. See a general account of the calamities, occasioned by the late tremendous hurricanes and earthquakes in the West-Indian islands, by Mr. Fowler.

118 The many ships of war belonging to the British navy, which were lost with all their crews in these dreadful hurricanes, will sufficiently prove the fact.

Also from Benediction Books ...
Wandering Between Two Worlds:
Essays on Faith and Art
Anita Mathias
Benediction Books, 2007
152 pages
ISBN: 0955373700

Available from www.amazon.com, www.amazon.co.uk

In these wide-ranging lyrical essays, Anita Mathias writes, in lush, lovely prose, of her naughty Catholic childhood in Jamshedpur, India; her large, eccentric family in Mangalore, a sea-coast town converted by the Portuguese in the sixteenth century; her rebellion and atheism as a teenager in her Himalayan boarding school, run by German missionary nuns, St. Mary's Convent, Nainital; and her abrupt religious conversion after which she entered Mother Teresa's convent in Calcutta as a novice. Later rich, elegant essays explore the dualities of her life as a writer, mother, and Christian in the United States-- Domesticity and Art, Writing and Prayer, and the experience of being "an alien and stranger" as an immigrant in America, sensing the need for roots.

About the Author

Anita Mathias is the author of *Wandering Between Two Worlds: Essays on Faith and Art.* She has a B.A. and M.A. in English from Somerville College, Oxford University, and an M.A. in Creative Writing from the Ohio State University, USA. Anita won a National Endowment of the Arts fellowship in Creative Nonfiction in 1997. She lives in Oxford, England with her husband, Roy, and her daughters, Zoe and Irene.

Visit Anita's website
  http://www.anitamathias.com,
  and Anita's blog
http://dreamingbeneaththespires.blogspot.com, (Dreaming Beneath the Spires).

The Church That Had Too Much
Anita Mathias
Benediction Books, 2010
52 pages
ISBN: 9781849026567

Available from www.amazon.com, www.amazon.co.uk

The Church That Had Too Much was very well-intentioned. She wanted to love God, she wanted to love people, but she was both hampered by her muchness and the abundance of her possessions, and beset by ambition, power struggles and snobbery. Read about the surprising way The Church That Had Too Much began to resolve her problems in this deceptively simple and enchanting fable.

About the Author

Anita Mathias is the author of *Wandering Between Two Worlds: Essays on Faith and Art.* She has a B.A. and M.A. in English from Somerville College, Oxford University, and an M.A. in Creative Writing from the Ohio State University, USA. Anita won a National Endowment of the Arts fellowship in Creative Nonfiction in 1997. She lives in Oxford, England with her husband, Roy, and her daughters, Zoe and Irene.

Visit Anita's website
   Http://www.anitamathias.com,
   and Anita's blog
http://dreamingbeneaththespires.blogspot.com (Dreaming Beneath the Spires).

www.ingramcontent.com/pod-product-compliance
Lightning Source LLC
Chambersburg PA
CBHW030520100426
42813CB00001B/99